FREE VIDEO **FREE VIDEO**

Essential Test Tips Video from Trivium Test Prep!

Dear Customer,

Thank you for purchasing from Trivium Test Prep! We're honored to help you prepare for your SIFT exam.

To show our appreciation, we're offering a **FREE *SIFT Essential Test Tips* Video by Trivium Test Prep**.* Our video includes 35 test preparation strategies that will make you successful on the SIFT. All we ask is that you email us your feedback and describe your experience with our product. Amazing, awful, or just so-so: we want to hear what you have to say!

To receive your **FREE *SIFT Essential Test Tips* Video**, please email us at 5star@ triviumtestprep.com. Include "Free 5 Star" in the subject line and the following information in your email:

1. The title of the product you purchased.

2. Your rating from 1 – 5 (with 5 being the best).

3. Your feedback about the product, including how our materials helped you meet your goals and ways in which we can improve our products.

4. Your full name and shipping address so we can send your **FREE *SIFT Essential Test Tips* Video**.

If you have any questions or concerns please feel free to contact us directly at 5star@triviumtestprep.com.

Thank you!

- Trivium Test Prep Team

*To get access to the free video please email us at 5star@triviumtestprep.com, and please follow the instructions above.

SIFT Test Study Guide

Comprehensive Review with Practice Test Questions for the U.S. Army's Selection Instrument for Flight Training Exam

Copyright © 2020 by Accepted, Inc.

ALL RIGHTS RESERVED. By purchase of this book, you have been licensed one copy for personal use only. No part of this work may be reproduced, redistributed, or used in any form or by any means without prior written permission of the publisher and copyright owner. Accepted, Inc.; Trivium Test Prep; Cirrus Test Prep; and Ascencia Test Prep are all imprints of Trivium Test Prep, LLC.

USAREC was not involved in the creation or production of this product, is not in any way affiliated Accepted, Inc., and does not sponsor or endorse this product. All test names (or their acronyms) are trademarks of their respective owners. This study guide is for general information and does not claim endorsement by any third party.

Questions regarding permissions or copyrighting may be sent to support@acceptedinc.com.

Table of Contents

INTRODUCTION

The SIFT exam, or "Selection Instrument for Flight Training" is utilized by the Army to determine if candidates are qualified for selection for flight officer training programs. The exam is designed to test multiple different aspects of potential candidates, which is intended to be predictors of training performance. Some of the sections might not seem to have anything to do with actual aviation, but another goal of the exam is to determine overall academic ability and essentially how hard you are willing to work for it or not. In short: how smart are you and do you possess the drive and motivation required to be a leader in the US Army.

Sections on the SIFT

There are 7 sections on the SIFT as follows:
1. Simple Drawings (SD) – 2 minutes, 100 questions
2. Hidden Figures (HF) – 5 minutes, 50 questions
3. Army Aviation Information Test (AAIT) – 30 minutes, 40 questions
4. Spatial Apperception Test (SAT) – 10 minutes, 25 questions
5. Reading Comprehension Test (RCT)– 30 minutes, 20 questions
6. Math Skills Test (MST) – 40 minutes, test length varies
7. Mechanical Comprehension Test (MCT) – 15 minutes, test length varies
8. From the time you check in for the exam, count on the entire exam lasting approximately 3 hours, although many test-takers often complete the exam in about 2 hours. We will cover each section in detail in the following chapters of this book, each followed up with practice questions like those you will see on the SIFT exam.

Scoring on the SIFT

Scores range from 20-80 with a 40 being a passing score. The low 50's is an average score. Obviously, you want to try to do better than that since the selection process is a competitive one, although there is varied reports of whether or not boards actually see your score or just that you passed without indicator of actual score. Either way, you should not treat test-day as a "trial run" and study hard now. You are only allowed take the SIFT twice in your life!

Additional Test Information

The most important sections to study for are those that lend themselves to be studied. Kind of a confusing statement, right? What is meant by that is of the 7 sections, you should devote a majority of your study time to three of them: Math Skills, Mechanical Comprehension, and Army Aviation Information. These sections will have the most bang for your buck for study effort, especially since many test-takers probably haven't studied math or physics (as found in the Mechanical Comprehension section) for many years, and very possibly have zero real-world experience with aviation.

The other 4 sections (Simple Drawings, Hidden Figures, Spatial Apperception, and Reading Comprehension) you need to familiarize yourself with and move on, as these sections you cannot "study" much beyond that. Your objective in preparation for these sections is just to make sure the first time you see them isn't on test day.

Overall, you should only spend a few hours in combined total studying for Simple Drawings, Hidden Figures, Spatial Apperception, and Reading Comprehension. Many will find they only spend 1 or 2 hours on them...maybe even less. The rest of your time should be devoted to the other three sections as they are more substantially more difficult, more academically driven (as opposed to "skills" like the other sections), cover more material, and will result in higher scores for your study effort.

Additional Resources

Keep in mind that while the SIFT is a relatively new test (introduced in 2013), many of the sections were picked up from the AFOQT for the Air Force and ASTB for the Naval forces. While the number of questions and time limits are different, you can find a plethora of practice tests and helpful information on discussion forums online.

Be certain to visit www.usarec.army.mil and find your way to the SIFT FAQs… or just Google "SIFT exam" or "SIFT FAQ" and it will be the very first result. This is the official information about the SIFT exam and you should read it carefully.

Testing Strategies

There are two very different strategies you will have to utilize on the SIFT exam as there are two different types of subtest sections you will encounter.

The first are the "fixed number of questions" sections: Simple Drawings, Hidden Figures, Army Aviation Information Test, Spatial Apperception, and Reading Comprehension. On these sections, any question left unanswered is counted as incorrect, which simply means, don't leave a single question unanswered! If you see time is running out, guess on every question before the clock runs down. Also on these sections, you can go skip questions or go back later, so if time permits, check your work before moving on.

The second type of subtest is the "Computer Adaptive" type. This is only for the Math Skills and Mechanical Comprehension. Under no circumstances should you ever guess without first giving your very best effort on these sections. The reasons are two-fold: 1) you cannot go back and change answers later. 2) the "Adaptive" word means that each test is customized to each test taker. As you answer questions, depending on whether or not you answer them correctly or not will determine the question you get next. If you get a question right, the next question will be more difficult. If you get it wrong, the next one will be easier. Each time you get a wrong answer, you maximum possible score drops lower and lower. Blindly guessing will significantly decrease the possibility of even passing this section, because after too many wrong answers you essentially fail automatically. This is why the test lengths vary, because if you get 5 or 10 questions in row correct, they know you are good to go and you can move on. If you miss 5 or 10 in a row, they know you don't have a prayer of passing so don't bother giving you any more chances.

Chapter One: Simple Drawings

As indicated in the name, this section is simple. So simple in fact, you should not spend more than about 10 minutes "studying" for this section. No, we are not kidding. In fact, most people will only need about 90 seconds. In fact, it isn't even really possible to "study", but only familiarize yourself with how this test section is designed and what you need to do.

You will have a mere 120 seconds to answer 100 questions in which you select a shape or object that is not like the other shape or objects. The questions are so simple however, that a pre-kindergartner could answer them. No, again, we aren't kidding. A 3 or 4 year old could answer these questions....maybe not necessarily as quickly as you can, but the point remains. As you noticed though, the trick is not in the difficulty (or lack thereof) of the questions themselves, but the fact that no one can possibly answer all 100 in the short amount of time allotted: 1.2 seconds per question.

The best way to prepare for this section is to just run through some practice questions. We gave you a quarter of the actual test length to see what it is like. Get a stop-watch or pull up a timer on your phone and go through all 25 as fast as possible without sacrificing accuracy. This will give you a rough idea of how many questions you will be able to answer on the actual test. Once you've done that....move on to the other sections!

You can theoretically "guess" on this test section if time is running out, but we advise against it. The better strategy in this instance is to just answer as many correctly as possible. Let's say you have 10 seconds left on the clock. You could just click "A" for every answer as fast as possible and get through 10 or maybe even 15 of them if you are lucky. You have a 20% chance (1 in 5) of answering correctly, so you would have statistically answered 2 or 3 correctly. Most test-takers typically are able to answer in the range of 70-85 questions in the Simple Drawings section. That means on average, it takes them 1.4 to 1.7 seconds per question. That means in the remaining 10 seconds, most people will be able to correct answer 5 to 7 more questions.

The bottom line? Try it out now and time yourself so you know what to expect on test day and have a ballpark of your speed in questions/second. On test day, do not even look at the clock. Each glance at the clock could eat up another potentially answered question.

Simple Drawings Practice Test

1.

A.	B.	C.	D.	E.
□	□	□	□	■

2.

A.	B.	C.	D.	E.
=	=	=	=	⩾

3.

A.	B.	C.	D.	E.
⊕	⬬	⬬	⬬	⬬

4.

A.	B.	C.	D.	E.
⇧	⇧	⇧	⬆	⇧

5.

A.	B.	C.	D.	E.

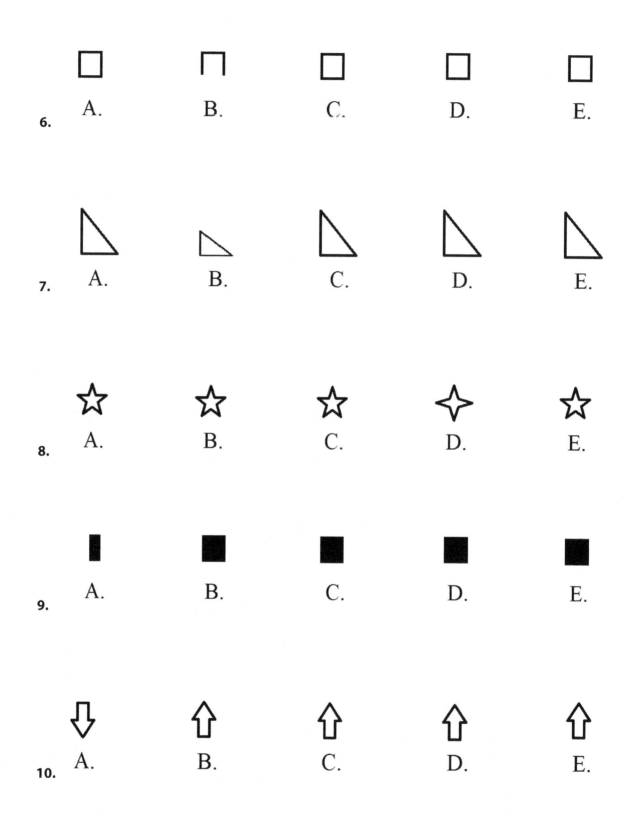

6. A. B. C. D. E.

7. A. B. C. D. E.

8. A. B. C. D. E.

9. A. B. C. D. E.

10. A. B. C. D. E.

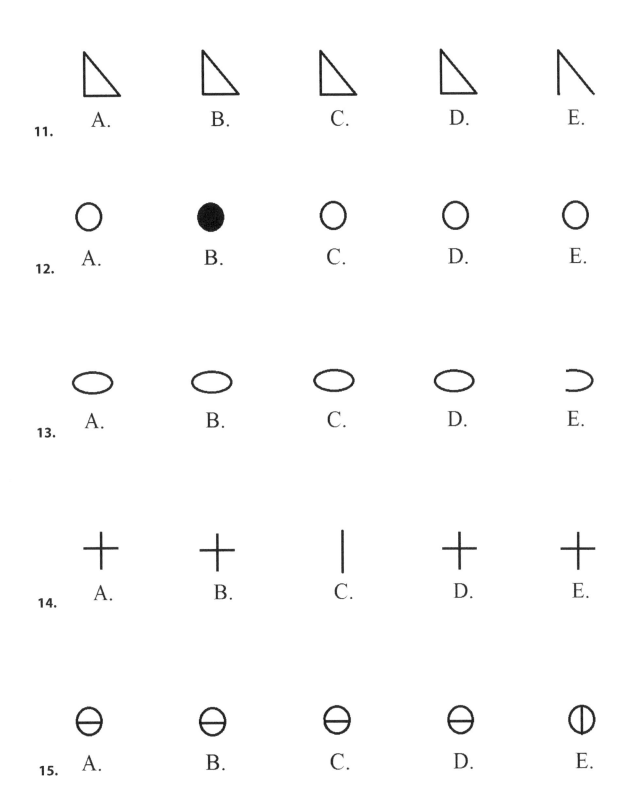

11. A.   B.   C.   D.   E.

12. A.   B.   C.   D.   E.

13. A.   B.   C.   D.   E.

14. A.   B.   C.   D.   E.

15. A.   B.   C.   D.   E.

11

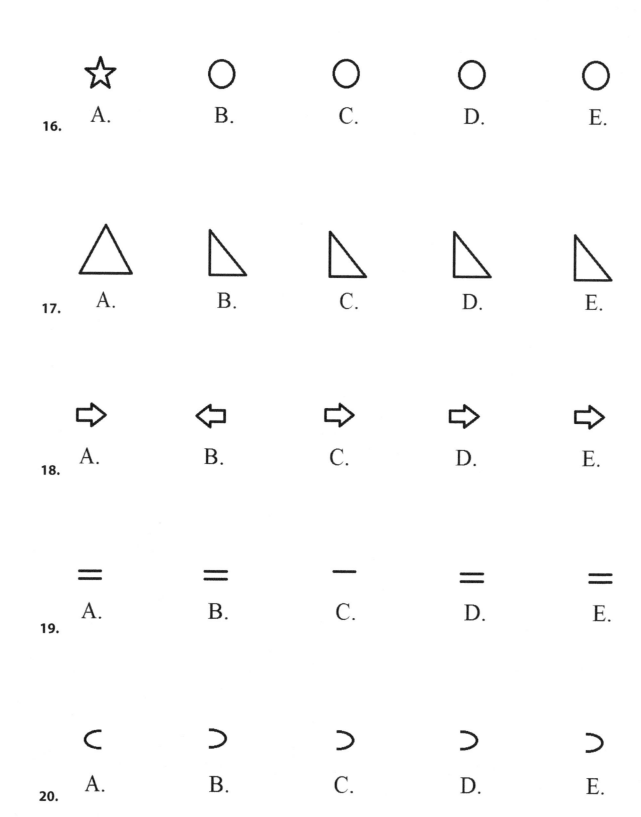

16. A.   B.   C.   D.   E.

17. A.   B.   C.   D.   E.

18. A.   B.   C.   D.   E.

19. A.   B.   C.   D.   E.

20. A.   B.   C.   D.   E.

12

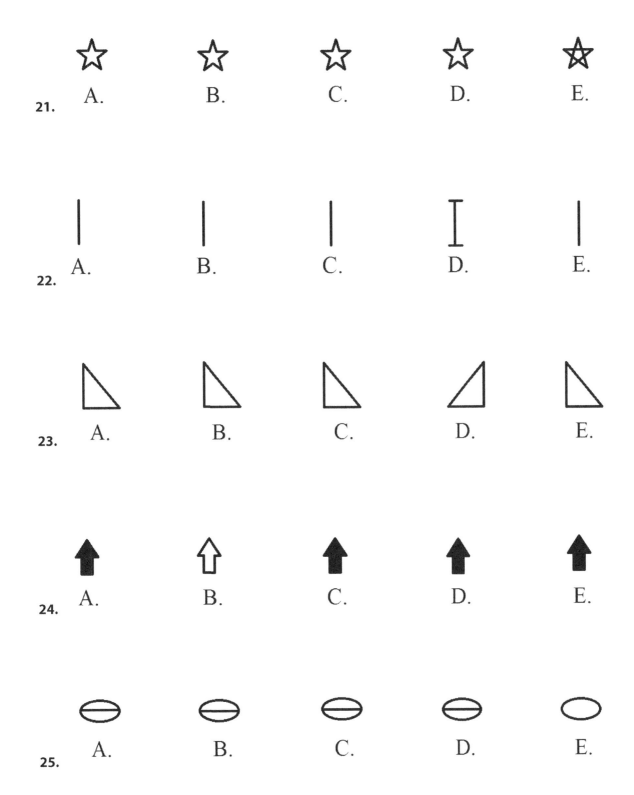

21. A.   B.   C.   D.   E.

22. A.   B.   C.   D.   E.

23. A.   B.   C.   D.   E.

24. A.   B.   C.   D.   E.

25. A.   B.   C.   D.   E.

1. E.
2. E.
3. A.
4. D.
5. B.
6. B.
7. B.
8. D.
9. A.
10. A.
11. E.
12. B.
13. E.
14. C.
15. E.
16. A.
17. A.
18. B.
19. C.
20. A.
21. E.
22. D.
23. D.
24. B.
25. E.

Chapter Two: Hidden Figures

In the hidden figures section, you will have 5 minutes to complete 50 items. The first thing you will notice about this section is the formatting of the questions is totally different than any other section. You will be given 5 shapes with correlating answer choices A, B, C, D, & E. Below those answer choices, you will be presented the questions which is a box with a lot of zig-zagging lines in all directions. Somewhere in those zig-zagged lines is a shape that matches one of the 5 answer choices.

This section is straightforward enough, but a few things to remember that can help you:

❖ First and foremost, it is imperative to remember that the shape in the hidden figure will always match the same size, position, and orientation as shown in the answer choice selections. Do not over-analyze and think you see a figure that is rotated 90 degrees or slightly bigger or smaller because the SIFT will never present questions that way on this section.

❖ Find a defining feature of the answer choices. That one long section or sharply angled protrusion can help you quickly ID the shape in many cases.

❖ Speed is essential here. You have 6 seconds per question, so you need to move through the questions with a purpose and never linger on a question for too long. That said, don't rush because the objective is to answer the questions correctly, not to see how fast you can click.

❖ Finally, this works for some and not for others…but if you squint and almost blur out the hidden figure image a little, sometimes the shapes will just kind of "appear" because there is a pattern to them, whereas the other lines in the box are just meant to distract and conceal. Not very scientific, we know, but this has been a life-saver for many people.

Let's get started with some practice on the next page. Do not let the hidden figure section overwhelm you. Even if you are struggling with it, just get familiar with how this section looks so you know what to expect on test day, but focus your attention on the other sections as they are more important, require more study time, and you will see more results from your study effort.

Hidden Figures Practice Test

For questions 1-5, use the below shapes as answer choices:

A.

B.

C.

D.

E.

1.

2.

3.

4.

5.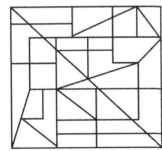

For questions 6-10, use the below shapes as answer choices:

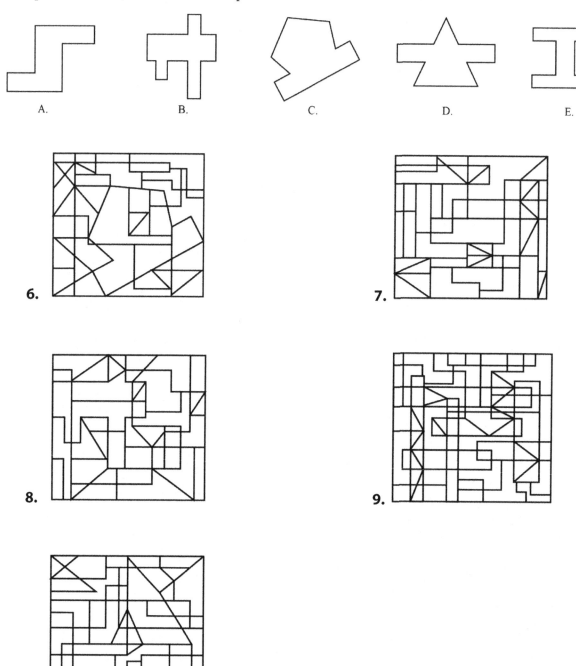

A.

B.

C.

D.

E.

6.

7.

8.

9.

10.

18

For questions 11-15, use the below shapes as answer choices:

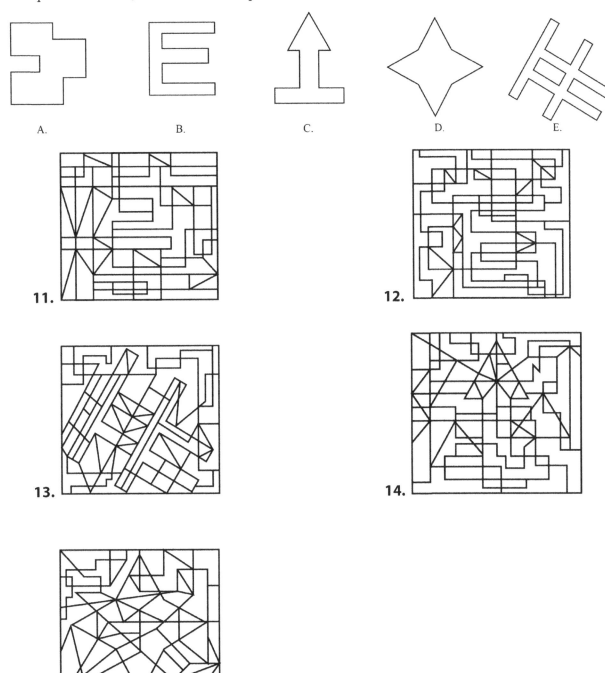

A.

B.

C.

D.

E.

11.

12.

13.

14.

15.

19

1. E.
2. B.
3. C.
4. D.
5. A.
6. C.
7. A.
8. B.
9. E.
10. D.
11. A.
12. B.
13. E.
14. C.
15. D.

Chapter Three: Army Aviation Information Test

The Army Aviation Information Test (AAIT) allows for 30 minutes to answer 40 multiple choice questions about aviation and helicopters in specific. If you have aviation experience such as private pilot's license, you are ahead of the curve but will still need to do some in depth studying as much of this information is technical and not so much about actually flying a plane. Unless you consider yourself an aviation expert already, you will need to study regardless of your current capability. Even those with PPL's report that this section was tough and required substantial studying effort.

A lot of information about helicopters is online. For example, the website of the Federal Aviation Administration (faa.gov) includes a 198-page, downloadable document, "Helicopter Flying Handbook." It is extremely important to download this resource and study it in depth. YouTube also has instructional videos about helicopters that can be quite helpful to better visualize and understand the concepts needed for this section.

Helicopter Structure and Components

During the past century, there have been many rotary-wing aircraft designed and built, including more than 400 types of helicopters. A helicopter is a type of rotorcraft that is able to take off and land vertically, hover, and fly forward, backward, and side to side (laterally). It can do so because it is equipped with a source of thrust: an engine that produces power and delivers it to overhead and tail rotors (on most helicopters) via one or more transmissions and drive shafts.

Helicopter engines are either piston or turbine; the advantage of the latter over the former is more thrust per pound.

Looking at a helicopter, we see a main body (fuselage) with a shaft (mast) protruding from the top. On the upper part of the fuselage of many helicopters is a cowling (shaped metal skin) that covers the aircraft's engine and transmission. Some helicopters have the engines externally mounted.

Depending on the type of helicopter, between two and six rotor blades are attached to the mast via a rotor head, which consists of several components, including a stabilizer bar (also called a flybar). The main rotor involves a complex swashplate mechanical system, which translate inputs from the pilot via the helicopter's flight controls into blade movement. Rotor system components include upper and lower swashplates, blade grips, control rods, pitch and scissor links, teeter or coning hinges, pitch horns, and counterweights.

The flybar's function is to enhance flight stability by keeping the bar stable as the rotor spins, and to reduce crosswind thrust on the blades. Through mechanical linkages, the bar's rotation combines with the swashplate's movement to damp internal (steering) and external (wind) forces on the rotor. The mechanical device makes it easier for the pilot to control the helicopter.

To provide additional stability, many helicopters have a horizontal stabilizer located roughly half way along the tail boom. The stabilizer helps to level the aircraft during forward flight.

Aft of the fuselage is a tail boom, which contains a drive shaft for the tail rotor, which is installed on the fin at the end of the helicopter. Tail rotors have two or more blades, depending on the size of the aircraft. They spin in the vertical plane, while the main, overhead rotor spins in an adjustable horizontal plane.

Some tail rotor tips are covered by a shroud made of formed metal or another durable material. The assembly is known as a ducted fan and the design reduces the possibility of someone walking into the spinning rotor blades and being injured or killed. The U.S. Coast Guard's Eurocopter HH-65 Dolphin is an example of a ducted fan helicopter.

Attached to the underside of many types of helicopters are a pair of skids that parallel the aircraft's longitudinal (nose-to-tail) axis. Some rotary-wing aircraft such as the U.S. Army's AH-64 Apache helicopter have wheels that hang down below the fuselage to absorb the weight of the aircraft when it is on the ground. Other helicopters have retractable wheels (called landing gear).

In a helicopter's cockpit are the pilots' seats, flight instruments and controls (cyclic, collective, throttle, and pedals), avionics (electronics used for navigation, communications, and aircraft systems), weapons controls (in military helicopters), and other equipment (e.g., fire extinguisher, flashlight).

Aerodynamics Forces

There are four main aerodynamic forces that act on a helicopter when it is airborne: weight, lift, thrust, and drag.

Everything on a helicopter – the aircraft's structure and components, pilots, fuel, cargo, etc. – has *weight*. Because of the earth's gravitational pull, the combined mass of a helicopter and its contents acts downward. From a physics perspective, the total weight force is deemed to act through a helicopter's center of gravity.

Aerodynamic loads associated with flight maneuvers and air turbulence affect the aircraft's weight. Whenever a helicopter flies a curved flight path at a certain altitude, the load factor (force of gravity, or "G") exerted on the rotor blades is greater than the aircraft's total weight.

When a pilot turns a helicopter by banking it, the amount of "G" increases. Banking more in order to turn more tightly causes the aircraft's weight to increase further. A helicopter banked 30 degrees weighs an additional 16 percent, but at 60 degrees of bank – a very steep turn – the aircraft weighs twice as much as it does in straight and level flight in smooth air.

Gusts produced by turbulent air can suddenly increase the angle of attack (AOA) of the rotor blades, which enlarges the load factor acting on them.

Lift is the force that counteracts an aircraft's weight and causes a helicopter to rise into the air and stay aloft. Lift is produced by airfoils – rotor blades, in the case of helicopters – that move through the air at a speed sufficient to create a pressure differential between the two sides of the airfoils. Lift acts perpendicular to the direction of flight through the airfoil's center of pressure, or center of lift.

Thrust is an aircraft's forward force, which is created by one or more engines (there are three in some rotary-wing machines), and is transformed in the case of helicopters into rotary motion via the components mentioned (transmission, drive shafts, rotor head, blades). Generally, thrust acts parallel to the aircraft's longitudinal axis, but not always.

Drag opposes thrust; it is a rearward-acting force caused by airflow passing over the aircraft's structure and becoming disrupted. Drag acts parallel to the relative wind. There are three types of drag that act on aircraft: profile, induced, and parasite.

As the main and tail rotors spin and the helicopter accelerates, *profile drag* created by the blades' frictional resistance increases. Profile drag consists of skin friction created by surface imperfections and form drag; the latter is caused by wake turbulence, airflow separating from the surface of an aircraft structure and creating eddies. The amount of form drag is a function of the size and shape of the structure as it protrudes into the relative wind.

Induced drag is created by air circulating around each rotor blade as it spins and creates lift; the circulation causes a vortex behind each blade. There is also a downward deflection of the airstream. As more lift is produced, induced drag and rotor downwash both increase. As well, increasing the AOA of the rotor blades, a technique used to increase lift, results in stronger vortices and greater induced drag. Because helicopters need a lot of lift, particularly at low speeds and while hovering, a high AOA during takeoff and initial climb and final approach and landing results in the greatest induced drag. Conversely, at cruising airspeeds when the rotor blades' AOA is shallow, induced drag is relatively small.

Parasite drag is created by helicopter components and attached equipment that do not contribute to lift, including the fuselage and tail section, skids or wheels, externally mounted engines, sensors, and weapons. These structures create a loss of airstream momentum proportional to their size and greater parasite drag at higher airspeeds. In fact, parasite drag varies with the square of the aircraft's velocity, so doubling the airspeed quadruples this type of drag.

A helicopter's *total drag*, which can be plotted on a graph as a curve, with airspeed on the other axis, is the sum of its profile, induced, and parasite drag. The curve's low point is the intersection of a certain airspeed and the smallest total drag. In other words, it is the point where the helicopter's lift-to-drag ratio (L/DMAX) is the greatest. At this speed, the total lift capacity is maximized, an aspect of helicopter performance of singular importance to pilots.

Relevant Scientific Principles

Bernoulli's Principle

In 1738, a Swiss scientist named Daniel Bernoulli published a book entitled *Hydrodynamica* in which he explained that an increase of the inviscid flow of a fluid (i.e., the flow of an ideal, zero-viscosity liquid or gas) resulted in a decrease of fluid pressure. Bernoulli's famous equation is $P + \frac{1}{2}\rho v^2$ = a constant, where P = pressure (a force exerted divided by the area exerted upon); ρ (the Greek letter "rho") = the fluid's density; and v = the fluid's velocity.

The constant in Bernoulli's formula is derived from the scientific principle that energy cannot be created or destroyed – only its form can be changed – and a system's total energy does not increase or decrease.

Conservation of Energy

Bernoulli's Principle is based on the conservation of energy, which says that in a steady flow the sum of all forms of mechanical energy – a fluid's potential energy plus its kinetic energy – along a streamline (e.g., a tube) is the same at all points. Thus, greater fluid flow rate (higher speed) results in increased kinetic energy and dynamic pressure and reduced potential energy and static pressure.

A helicopter filled with fuel has a finite amount of energy. Through combustion in the engine, the fuel's heat energy is converted to kinetic energy through the transmission. If a helicopter were to be airborne when it ran out of fuel, the only energy left would be potential energy, a function of the aircraft's height above the ground. As the pilot nosed the helicopter down in order to keep air flowing over the rotor blades, a maneuver called autorotation, the aircraft's potential energy would be converted into kinetic energy.

Combining Bernoulli's Principle with the fact that helicopters have blades (airfoils) that spin and provide lift at varying speeds during different phases of flight (takeoff, climb, cruise, descent, landing), the lift produced in a given instant can be calculated using the following equation: $L = \frac{1}{2}\rho v^2 A C_l$, where L = the lift force, $\frac{1}{2}\rho v2$ was previously explained, A = the airfoil's area (length multiplied by width), and C_l is the coefficient of lift of the rotor blades.

Pilots must remember that the lifting force on their aircraft is proportional to the density (ρ) of air through which they fly (higher altitude = less dense air), the aircraft's speed, and airfoil AOA.

Venturi Effect

To understand how spinning rotor blades can produce enough force to lift a helicopter off the ground, climb, and maintain a cruising altitude, and how a moving tail rotor is able to generate a sideways, anti-torque force, we need to examine a phenomenon called the Venturi Effect.

In the late 18th century, an Italian physicist, Giovanni Battista Venturi, conducted experiments with a pump and an unusual tube. The diameter of one end of the tube was constant, while the circumference of the tube's central portion was smaller. Downstream from the bottleneck, the tube's diameter increased. It was as though someone had squeezed the center of the tube, creating a constriction.

Venturi noticed that as fluids moved through the tube, the flow rate increased (accelerated) and the force (static pressure) against the tube's surface decreased as the diameter became smaller. The opposite also happened: increasing tube diameter downstream resulted in reduced flow rate (deceleration) and greater static pressure. Venturi published his findings in 1797 and the effect that he observed, measured, and wrote about became associated with his name. It has certainly been integral to aviation since the development of gliding in the 19th century.

If a Venturi tube is cut in half longitudinally, the curvature of the tube wall would look similar to that of the top of a helicopter's rotor blade or an airplane's wing, which is also an airfoil. When a helicopter rotor blade spins, it "slices" the air, forcing molecules to travel along one side of the airfoil or the other. Those moving across the curved side have to travel a greater distance to reach the trailing edge than those moving across the relatively flat side. Consequently, the air molecules moving across the curved surface accelerate, as they did in Venturi's tube, and the static pressure drops.

Because pressure flows from high to low, the static pressure differential experienced between the two sides of rotating helicopter blades results in a force exerted on each airfoil from the high-pressure (flat) side to the low-pressure (curved) surface. In this way, lift is generated by the main rotor, and an anti-torque force acting perpendicular to the helicopter's longitudinal axis is created by the tail rotor (a smaller version of the overhead rotor turned vertically, essentially).

Newton's Third Law of Motion

Sir Isaac Newton (1642–1727) was a brilliant English physicist and mathematician who formulated universal laws of motion, including his third, which stated: "When one body exerts a force on a second body, the second body simultaneously exerts a force equal in magnitude and opposite in direction to that of the first body."

Rotor blades on helicopters designed and built in the United States, Canada, Britain, and Germany move in a counter-clockwise direction when viewed from above, and clockwise on rotary-wing aircraft made in Russia and other countries. Because of Newton's Third Law of Motion, the torque effect of the spinning main rotor is to rotate the aircraft in the opposite direction. To prevent this undesirable rotation, a sideways, anti-torque force is created on most helicopters by the spinning a tail rotor.

Alternatively, to eliminate torque counter-rotating rotors are used on other types of helicopters. Examples include the Boeing CH-47 Chinook (tandem rotors), Kaman K-1200 K-MAX (intermeshing rotors), and Kamov Ka-50 "Black Shark" (coaxial rotors).

Flight Controls

As mentioned, a helicopter has four controls that allow the pilot to maneuver the aircraft: the cyclic, collective, throttle, and pedals.

The *cyclic* control, which is typically called the "cyclic" or "cyclic stick", is located in front of the pilot(s) in the cockpit. It is similar to a joystick used to play video games in that it moves in all directions except up and down. By moving the control, the pilot varies the pitch of the main rotor blades on a cyclical basis (i.e., every revolution) via the complex rotor head system. The rotor head has been designed so that all blades have the same angle of incidence (explained later) at the same point during each revolution (cycle).

Moving the cyclic results in a change of blade angle of attack, thus generating variable lift as each blade spins around the mast. Blades rise or fall in sequence due to increasing or decreasing

AOA. For example, if the pilot moves the cyclic forward, the aft part of the rotor disk rises because of greater aft blade AOA, while the front drops. The result is a forward-tilting disk and a corresponding thrust vector imparted to the helicopter, which moves forward.

The *collective* is on the left side of the pilot's seat, moves up and down, and can be adjusted in terms of its position via a variable friction lock to prevent unwanted movement. Adjusting the collective alters the AOA of all the main rotor blades simultaneously, irrespective of their position. Pulling up on the collective increases blade AOA and aircraft climb rate; lowering it has the opposite effect.

In many helicopters, the *throttle*, which controls the power produced by the engine and rotates like a motorcycle throttle, is located at the end of the collective. In some turbine helicopters, the throttle control is mounted on the cockpit floor or an overhead panel. Single-engine helicopters typically have the motorcycle-style twist grip, while helicopters with two or more powerplants have a throttle lever for each engine.

Helicopter anti-torque *pedals* are located on the floor in front of the pilot(s) and used to control yaw (i.e., where the aircraft is pointing). Stepping on the left or right pedal causes the AOA of the tail rotor blades to change accordingly, altering the horizontal thrust vector created by the aft spinning airfoils. Viewed from above, the amount of horizontal "lift" (the sideways-acting force) generated by the tail rotor increases or decreases with pedal movement, changing the turning moment (force) acting on the helicopter in opposition to the torque force previously explained. As the tail moves left or right, the aircraft's nose moves in the opposite direction. When the pilot wants the helicopter's nose to move left or right, he or she pushes on the corresponding pedal.

Additional Helicopter Terms, Definitions, and Explanations

Advancing blade: As the main rotor spins, with each revolution the blades move either toward the front of the helicopter or its tail. In the case of the former, each blade advances, and doing so increases the relative wind speed across the airfoil. Consequently, lift increases and the blade moves (flaps) upward.

Airflow in forward flight: When a helicopter flies forward, air flows in a direction opposite to that of the aircraft, with a speed equal to the machine's forward velocity. Because the rotor spins, the speed of air flowing across each blade depends on the airfoil's position in the plane of rotation and the helicopter's airspeed. With each revolution, the longitudinal velocity vector of each blade is sometimes with the aircraft's forward speed and sometimes against it.

Consequently, the airflow meeting each blade varies as a function of its position in the circular movement cycle. For helicopters with a main rotor that spins counter-clockwise, the maximum airflow speed happens when the blade reaches the three o'clock (right) position. As the blade passes over the aircraft's forward fuselage and nose, the speed decreases. The lowest airflow velocity happens when the blade reaches the nine o'clock (left) position. As the blade crosses the helicopter's tail, airflow speed increases to rotor spin (rotational) velocity and then accelerates as the blade moves toward the right side.

Airfoil: An airfoil is a surface that generates lift greater than drag as air flows over the upper and lower surfaces. Helicopter main rotor and tail rotor blades are examples of airfoils, as is the horizontal stabilizer. Airfoils are carefully designed and can be made of non-metallic materials such as composites.

Angle of attack: The angle between the chord line of an airfoil (e.g., a rotor blade) and the airfoil's direction of motion relative to the air (the relative wind). AOA is an aerodynamic angle.

Angle of incidence: The angle between the chord line of each blade and the rotor system's plane of rotation (e.g., level, tilted). AOI is a mechanical angle.

Autorotation: A situation where the main rotor generates lift not because of a functioning engine, but solely because air flows across the blades is called autorotation. When a helicopter engine fails, a clutch mechanism called a freewheeling unit automatically disconnects the engine from the main rotor, allowing the latter to spin freely. During autorotation, the helicopter descends, causing air to flow across the blades and continuing to provide lift as they spin in the airstream.

Learning to perform an autorotation to a successful landing is an important part of helicopter pilot training and must be demonstrated to an inspector in order to obtain the desired certification. To be certified with civil or military aviation authorities, helicopters must have a freewheeling unit that allows for autorotation.

Autorotation (during forward flight): During an autorotation when the helicopter is moving forward, the rotor disk takes in upward flowing air and the driven, driving, and stall regions of each blade move outboard along its length (span), but only on the retreating side of the disk. With a lower AOA on the advancing blade, the driven region expands, while on the retreating blade, the stall region enlarges. Also, reversed airflow occurs in a small section near the root of the retreating blade, reducing the driven region.

Autorotation (while hovering): During an autorotation in a hover (in still air), dissymmetry of lift due to helicopter speed is not a factor because the forces that cause the blades to spin are similar for all the airfoils, regardless of whether they are advancing or retreating. The force vectors acting in the driven, driving, and stall regions of each blade are different because the rotational relative wind is slower near the blade root and greater toward the blade tip. Also, there is a smaller AOA in the driven region compared to the driving region due to blade twist. Inflow of air up through the rotor combined with the rotational relative wind creates varying aerodynamic forces at every point along the blade.

In the driven region during an autorotation while hovering, some lift is produced, but it is offset by drag due to the total aerodynamic force (TAF) acting aft of the axis of rotation. The net result is rotor deceleration. The size of the driven region varies with the number of rotor revolutions per minute (rpm), blade pitch, and the rate of descent.

TAF in the driving region – also called the autorotative region – is angled slightly forward of the axis of rotation, resulting in an acceleration force that provides thrust and a blade rotation acceleration tendency. Rotor rpm, blade pitch, and rate of descent affect the driving region's size, which the pilot can control, thereby altering autorotative rpm.

The inner one-quarter of the rotor blade is the stall region and operates above the stall angle (the maximum AOA) during an autorotation while hovering. In this part of the rotor disk, drag is created that reduces blade rotation.

Blade flapping: Too much lift causes blade flapping. In a hover, the blade angle is such that lift and centrifugal forces balance out. However, if lift is increased (due to excessive airspeed of the advancing blades) and centrifugal force remains unchanged, the extra lift will cause the blade to move upward to a point where the lift and centrifugal forces are again in balance.

Blade span: The distance from the tip of the rotor blade to the center of the drive shaft (rotational center point).

Blade twist: Greater pitch angles toward the blade root where rotational velocity is relatively low and progressively shallower pitch angles toward the blade tip where rotational velocity is comparatively high describes the design feature known as blade twist. Its purpose is to distribute the lifting force more evenly along the airfoil, thereby smoothing out internal blade stresses.

Chord: The distance between the leading and trailing edges along the chord line is an airfoil's chord. If the blade is tapered, as viewed from above or below, the chord at its tip will be different than at its root. Average chord describes the average distance.

Chord line: An imaginary straight line from the airfoil's leading (front) edge to its trailing (aft) edge.

Coning: A spinning rotor creates centrifugal force (inertia) that pulls the blades outward from the hub. The inertia is proportional to the rotational speed. As the rotating blades produce lift – during takeoff, for example – centrifugal force combines with the upward lift force to create a slightly conical shape (when the rotor is viewed from the side).

Coning angle: The angle formed between spinning rotor blades and a plane perpendicular to the mast.

Coriolis Effect (Law of Conservation of Angular Momentum): The Coriolis Effect states that a rotating body spins at the same speed (angular momentum) unless an external force is applied to change the rotational velocity. Angular momentum is the rotational speed multiplied by the moment of inertia (mass times distance from the center of rotation squared). Also, angular acceleration and deceleration occurs as a spinning body's mass is moved closer to or farther away from the axis of rotation, respectively. The speed of the rotating mass changes proportionately with the square of the radius (the distance between the spinning body and the center of rotation).

In the context of helicopters, as coning occurs the rotor's diameter decreases. However, due to the law of conservation of angular momentum the blades' speed remains the same despite the fact that the tips now travel a shorter distance due to the smaller disk diameter. What changes is rotor rpm, which increases lift slightly.

Dissymmetry of lift: Different wind flow speeds across the advancing and retreating halves of the rotor disk result in a dissymmetry of lift. After a helicopter takes off, the relative wind speed experienced by the advancing blade is increased by the aircraft's forward speed, while the opposite occurs on the retreating blade (due to the machine's forward vector). Consequently, the advancing side of the rotor disk produces more lift than the retreating blade side.

Left uncorrected, this situation would cause the helicopter to become uncontrollable. To eliminate dissymmetry of lift, the main rotor blades flap and rotate automatically with each revolution. A semi-rigid rotor system (comprised of two blades, as is common on light helicopters) involves a teetering hinge, which allows the blades to flap as a unit; when one blade flaps down, the other blade flaps up. Rotor systems with three or more blades use a horizontal flapping hinge, which permits each blade to flap up and down as it rotates around the mast.

Driven region: Also called the propeller region, the driven region is nearest to the blade tips and normally consists of nearly one-third (30 percent) of the radius. The driven region tends to slow the rotor's spin due to drag resulting from the region's TAF, which is inclined slightly behind the axis of rotation.

Driving region: Also known as the autorotative region, the driving region is normally between a blade's driven and stall regions. The total aerodynamic force of the driving region is inclined slightly forward of the axis of rotation, supplying thrust and accelerating the blade's rotation.

Effective translational lift (ETL): Helicopters experience effective translational lift while transitioning to forward flight at about 16 to 24 knots. By the upper end of the speed range, the aircraft has managed to out-run the blade vortices created during takeoff and initial forward acceleration. During ETL, the rotor system begins to pass through air that is relatively undisturbed and the airflow becomes more horizontal, resulting in less downwash and induced drag. Also, efficiency of the rotor system and helicopter airspeed both increase during ETL and the machine accelerates toward the part of flight where L/DMAX occurs.

As the airspeed increases and translational lift becomes more effective, the aircraft's nose pitches up and the helicopter rolls to the right (with a rotor system spinning counter-clockwise), movements that must be corrected by the pilot. The machine's tendency to behave this way during ETL is the result of dissymmetry of lift, gyroscopic precession, and transverse flow effect. Once the helicopter has transitioned through ETL, the pilot must push forward and left on the cyclic to maintain a constant attitude of the rotor disk.

Forward flight: In steady forward flight, lift is offset by weight and the forces of thrust and drag are equal. When the tip-path (rotation) plane is tilted forward (due to the pilot pushing the cyclic forward), the total lift-thrust force, which consists of horizontal and vertical components, is also angled forward. Because of these horizontal components, as the helicopter moves forward it begins to lose altitude (due to the reduced vertical lift vector), a situation the pilot must correct.

As the helicopter begins to accelerate from a hover, translational lift causes the efficiency of the rotor system to increase, resulting in power in excess of that which was needed for hovering. Continued acceleration increases airflow and expands the excess power. Once the helicopter has reached its assigned or desired altitude and airspeed, the pilot reduces the power to maintain straight-and-level, unaccelerated flight, noting the torque (power) setting and not making any major changes to the flight controls.

Gyroscopic precession: When a force is applied to a spinning mass (e.g., a child's top, a helicopter rotor), the resulting effect occurs not at the point of force application, but 90 degrees later in the direction of rotation. In a helicopter, if a downward force is applied, say, on the starboard (right) side of the counter-clockwise-spinning rotor disk, the movement response occurs at the rotor's twelve o'clock position (i.e., in front of the fuselage). Wind gusts can apply such forces on rotors.

Hovering flight: One element of vertical flight is hovering. To hover a helicopter, the main rotor must produce lift equal to the aircraft's total weight. At high rotor rpm and increasing blade pitch (AOA) generate the lift required to hover. During hovering, rotor blade tip vortices reduce the effectiveness of the outer blade and negatively affect the lift of the following blades. For this reason, a lot of power is required during a hover.

Because of the helicopter's blade downwash (induced flow) while it is hovering, the velocity of air under the aircraft can reach 60 to 100 knots, depending on the rotor's diameter and the machine's size and weight.

During the hover, the relative wind and AOA are changed by the downward airflow and the TAF is reduced. Consequently, the pilot has to increase collective pitch (pull up on the collective) to create enough TAF to continue hovering. However, the increase in lift is accompanied by greater induced drag, so the total power needed to hover is greater, requiring the pilot to increase the engine throttle.

Induced flow (downwash): As rotor blades spin, they create rotational relative wind, airflow that is parallel as well as opposite to the rotor's plane of rotation and perpendicular to each blade's leading edge. As the blades rotate, air accelerates over the airfoils and is projected downward. Moving a large amount of air vertically and down through the rotor system, which occurs during takeoff and hover, creates induced flow, which can greatly alter the efficiency of the system. Rotational relative wind combines with downwash to form a resultant relative wind, which becomes more vertical as induced flow increases.

In ground effect (IGE): A "cushion" of air beneath moving airfoils (e.g., spinning rotor blades) and the takeoff/landing surface (e.g., a heliport deck) provides additional lift to the aircraft when it is close to the ground. During IGE, lift acts more vertically, induced drag is reduced, and the relative wind is more horizontal, all of which increases the efficiency of the rotor system. Maximum ground effect occurs during a hover above smooth, hard surfaces, up to a height equal to the main rotor's diameter.

Inherent sideslip: In forward flight, the tail rotor creates a sideward force and the helicopter slightly tilts to the wind when the main rotor disk is level and the slip ball in the pilot's turn-and-bank indicator is centered. The fin (vertical stabilizer) on larger helicopters is designed with the tail rotor mounted in such a way as to correct inherent sideslip. Also, installing the tail rotor on top of the fin places the anti-torque force vector closer to the horizontal plane of the main rotor's torque, reducing tilt when the aircraft is airborne.

Mean camber line: An imaginary line between the leading and trailing edges and halfway between the airfoil's upper (curved) and lower (relatively flat) surfaces.

Non-symmetrical airfoil (cambered): When one surface of an airfoil has a specific curvature that the opposite side does not, the airfoil is described as non-symmetrical, or cambered. The advantage of a non-symmetrical helicopter blade, for example, is that it produces lift at an AOA of zero degrees (as long as airflow is moving past the blade). Moreover, the lift-to-drag ratio and stall characteristics of a cambered airfoil are better than those of a symmetrical airfoil. Its disadvantages are center of the pressure movement chord-wise by as much as one-fifth the chord line distance, which causes undesirable blade torsion, and greater airfoil production costs.

Out of ground effect (OGE): Once a helicopter climbs to an altitude that exceeds the diameter of the main rotor, it is said to be out of ground effect. The IGE air "cushion" is gone and because the horizontal component of the relative wind decreases while induced drag increases, there is a decrease in lift. A greater blade angle is needed to maintain lift, but increasing the blade pitch also creates more drag. For this reason, increasing pitch while hovering in OGE requires more power than during an IGE hover. Also, under certain conditions there is a localized downward airflow that causes the helicopter to sink at an alarming rate, an effect called settling with power.

Pendular action: In terms of physics, a helicopter with a single main rotor is suspended from a single point in space and swings like a pendulum. Since a pilot can exacerbate pendular action by over-controlling the aircraft, he or she needs to fly using smooth control inputs.

Rearward flight: When the rotor disc is tilted rearward, flight in that direction occurs. In such a situation, the pilot must be mindful that the vertical component of the drag vector acts in the same direction as lift (up) and weight (down). Because the horizontal stabilizer on the tail boom is designed to function during forward, not rearward flight, when the latter occurs the likelihood of the tail skid striking the ground (at a very low altitude) increases. Also, with the pilot seated facing forward and the helicopter's skids (if so equipped) not curved upward on the aft end, rearward flight hazards are greater than when flying forward.

Relative wind: The flow of air in relation to a helicopter's blades is called the relative wind. It moves in a direction opposite to that of the aircraft and spinning rotor. Rotating helicopter blades experience a relative wind comprised of horizontal and vertical parts, the former resulting from the turning blades plus the aircraft's movement through the air, and the latter due to induced flow plus air movement as the helicopter climbs or descends.

Resultant relative wind: Airflow created by the rotor's spin and modified by induced flow (downwash) creates the resultant relative wind. When the helicopter is moving horizontally, the resultant relative wind changes with the aircraft's speed. The airspeed component of the relative wind is added to the rotational relative wind when the blade is advancing, and subtracted when the blade is retreating.

Retreating blade stall: As the helicopter's forward speed increases, the airspeed of the retreating blade decreases. However, to ensure aircraft flight stability the retreating blade needs to produce as much lift as the advancing blade. Therefore, the AOA of the retreating blade must be increased to augment lift in the retreating portion of the rotor disk. If the helicopter's forward speed reaches a value that exceeds the velocity associated with the maximum AOA of the retreating blade, it will stall (i.e., no longer generate lift).

When a rotor blade enters a stall, the pilot feels an abnormal vibration due to the loss of lift. A deepening stall results in the aircraft rolling and pitching nose up.

A blade stall is caused by high blade loading (due to high helicopter gross weight), low rotor rpm, operating at a high density altitude, steep or abrupt turns, and/or turbulent air.

With the onset of rotor blade stall, corrective action taken by the pilot involves reducing power (by lowering the collective), airspeed, and "G" loads during maneuvering; increasing rotor rpm to the maximum permitted; and checking pedal trim.

Rotational relative wind (tip-path plane): As rotor blades spin, they produce a rotational relative wind, as called tip-path plane. Rotational relative wind, which strikes a blade perpendicular to its leading edge and parallel to the plane of rotation, constantly changes as the rotor spins. The wind velocity is greatest at the tip of each blade and decreases to zero at the mast's center.

Rotor blade angles: Two rotor blade angles are key aspects of helicopter aerodynamics: angle of attack and angle of incidence.

Rotor system: A helicopter's rotor system consists of the following main components:
- o   Hub: the mechanical apparatus on the upper mast where the root of each rotor blade is installed.
- o   Tip: the rotor blade section farthest from the hub.
- o   Root: the part of the blade where it is attached to the hub.
- o   Twist: the change in angle designed and built into the blade from the root to the tip.

Settling with power: Also known as vortex ring state, settling with power occurs when a helicopter sinks into its own downwash. Settling with power involves a descent straight down or nearly vertical at a minimum of 300 feet per minute and low forward speed. As well, the main rotor system must be using between 20 and 100 percent of engine power, leaving – in some cases – insufficient power for the pilot to stop the sink rate.

Vortex ring state can occur during approaches with a tailwind or when there is turbulence caused by one or more nearby helicopters, as has happened during formation approaches.

Settling with power also creates a secondary vortex ring around each blade's point where airflow changes from up to down. The net result is turbulence over a considerable portion of the spinning blades, which causes a reduction of rotor efficiency despite the fact that the engine is still delivering power to the system.

Sideward flight: For a helicopter to fly sideways, the main rotor disc must be tilted in the desired direction, causing a sideways component of the lift vector to be generated and take effect on the aircraft. Because of parasite drag caused by the helicopter moving sideways through the air and the lack of a horizontal stabilizer for such movement, sideward flight can create a very unstable condition. The pilot needs to be aware of any obstruction to the left or right of the helicopter and bear in mind the relatively low position of the rotor disk edge at the three or nine o'clock position during sideward flight.

Stall region: The inboard one-quarter of the rotor blade is known as the stall region, which operates above the stall angle of attack and creates drag. The stall region tends to slow down the spinning rotor.

Symmetrical airfoil: When an airfoil has identical upper and lower surfaces, it is symmetrical and produces no lift at an AOA of zero degrees. The main rotor blades of most light helicopters are symmetrical.

Total aerodynamic force (TAF): Two components comprise the total aerodynamic force: lift and drag. The amount of lift and drag produced by an airfoil are primarily determined by its shape and area.

Translational lift: Enhanced rotor efficiency due to the helicopter transitioning from a hover to directional flight results in translational lift. The relative wind increases during directional flight acceleration, augmenting airflow across the rotor blades while the turbulence and vortices associated with hovering decrease.

Translating tendency (drift): A helicopter with one main rotor tends to drift in the direction of tail rotor thrust (i.e., laterally). The following features have been incorporated into helicopters (with a main rotor that spins counter-clockwise) to counteract the drifting tendency:

1. Tilting the rotor mast to the left (as viewed from behind the helicopter), which is accomplished by doing the same to the main transmission. The mast tilt opposes the tail rotor thrust responsible for the translating tendency.
2. Rigging the flight controls so that the main rotor disk is tilted slightly left when the cyclic is centered.

Translational thrust: While transitioning from hover to forward flight, relative wind flows across the tail rotor, increasing its aerodynamic efficiency, a phenomenon called translational thrust. As the tail rotor becomes more aerodynamically efficient, it produces greater anti-torque thrust, which results in the helicopter's nose yawing left (in a helicopter with a main rotor spinning counter-clockwise). To counteract the yaw, the pilot applies right pedal, decreasing the tail rotor blades' AOA.

Transverse flow effect: When accelerating in forward flight, induced flow (downwash) at the forward disk area decreases, while increasing in the aft disk area. The difference between the two rotor regions is called transverse flow effect. Because of the effect as well as gyroscopic precession, acceleration through about 20 knots or into a 20-knot headwind causes the helicopter (with a rotor that spins counter-clockwise) to roll to the right. Transverse flow effect is countered by the pilot moving the cyclic to the left.

Turning flight: In a banking turn, the rotor disk is tilted by movement of the cyclic to the left or right side, an action that creates a sideway component of the lift vector. This horizontal force – called the centripetal force – opposes inertia, or centrifugal force. As the bank angle increases, the centripetal force becomes greater, causing the turn rate to increase. However, the vertical component of the lift vector decreases. To compensate and maintain altitude, the pilot must enlarge the blades' AOA by increasing (pulling up on) the collective.

Vertical flight: To achieve vertical flight upward, the helicopter's lift and thrust must exceed its weight and drag. Increasing the main rotor blades' AOA while maintaining their rotational speed creates extra lift and the aircraft ascends. Decreasing the pitch results in a descent.

Vortex ring state: See Settling with power

Army Aviation Information Practice Test

1. A helicopter is:
   - **A.** A type of gyrocraft
   - **B.** A type of rotorcraft
   - **C.** A category of rotary-wing airplanes
   - **D.** A sub-group of gyrocopters

2. Helicopter turbine engines produce _____ thrust per pound than piston engines:
   - **A.** less
   - **B.** the same
   - **C.** more
   - **D.** the same, but only after factoring in the effect of density altitude

3. The main forces acting on a helicopter are:
   - **A.** Induced lift, mass, thrust, and form drag
   - **B.** Lift, weight, thrust, and drag
   - **C.** Lift, gravity, air resistance, and rotor vortex drag
   - **D.** None of the above

4. Helicopters typically have between __ and __ main rotor blade(s):
   - **A.** 2, 6
   - **B.** 2, 10
   - **C.** 3, 8
   - **D.** 3, 7

5. Depending on the type of helicopter, main rotor system components can include:
   - **A.** A stabilizer bar, upper and lower swashplates, and counterweights.
   - **B.** Pitch horns, teeter or coning hinges, and blade grips.
   - **C.** Pitch and scissor links, and control rods.
   - **D.** All of the above

6. The function of the flybar is:
   A. To decrease crosswind thrust on the blades and enhance flight stability by keeping the bar stable as the rotor spins
   B. To increase crosswind thrust and modify flight stability by allowing the bar to spin at a slower speed than the main rotor
   C. To decrease crosswind thrust and augment flight stability by maintaining the bar at an acute angle to the main rotor
   D. To spin in a direction opposite to the main rotor's, thereby reducing induced drag

7. Many helicopters have a horizontal stabilizer located:
   A. On the mast
   B. On the tail boom
   C. On the fin
   D. None of the above

8. The purpose of the tail rotor is:
   A. To create kinetic energy that is transformed into potential energy as the helicopter climbs
   B. To produce rotational momentum that is used by the transmission to drive a generator
   C. To produce an anti-torque force acting perpendicular to the helicopter's longitudinal axis
   D. All of the above

9. Wheels on _____ types of helicopters are _____:
   A. all, retractable (to reduce drag)
   B. some, supplementary to skids
   C. some, retractable
   D. all, supplementary to skids

10. A pilot controls a helicopter using:
   A. Flight instruments, hydraulic actuators, and a cyclic with a twist throttle
   B. Flight instruments, pedals, two or more throttle levers, and avionics
   C. Pedals, a throttle with a twist grip, collective link rods, and a cyclic
   D. Pedals, and a collective, throttle, and cyclic

11. From a physics perspective, the _____ force is deemed to act through a helicopter's
_____:
   A. lift, center of motion
   B. total weight, center of gravity
   C. induced drag, longitudinal axis
   D. total mass, center of motion

12. When a pilot banks a helicopter, causing it to turn, _____:
   A. The machine's weight increases.
   B. The machine's weight remains the same.
   C. The machine's gravitational drag increases.
   D. The vertical component of the lift vector remains the same.

13. In the case of helicopters, lift is produced by _____ moving through the air at a
speed sufficient to create _____:
   A. rotor blades, gyroscopic precession.
   B. the flybar, an anti-drag force.
   C. airfoils, a pressure differential.
   D. None of the above.

14. Thrust acts _____ to the aircraft's _____:
   A. at an acute angle, driven portion of the tail rotor disk.
   B. perpendicular, rotational relative wind.
   C. laterally, outer two-thirds of the main rotor disk.
   D. parallel, longitudinal axis.

15. Profile drag consists of _____ created by _____ and _____:
   A. induced drag, angular momentum, aircraft components that do not contribute to lift.
   B. skin friction, surface imperfections, form drag.
   C. an inclined main rotor disk, increasing angle of attack, high blade rpm.
   D. None of the above.

16. Vortices produced by spinning rotor blades create:
   A. Form drag.
   B. Rotational drag.
   C. Parasite drag.
   D. Induced drag.

17. When plotted on a graph, L/DMAX is the point where the helicopter's _____.

    A. Total lift-to-drag ratio is the greatest.

    B. Induced lift-to-drag ratio is maximized.

    C. Perpendicular lift component exceeds the rotational drag vector by at least 50 percent.

    D. Ability to carry pilots, cargo, etc. at the maneuvering speed is most fuel-efficient.

18. A helicopter's potential energy is affected by:

    A. The tail rotor's anti-torque force.

    B. The relative wind.

    C. The aircraft's height above the ground.

    D. All of the above.

19. Which of the following factors affect the lift produced by spinning rotor blades:

    A. Airfoil coefficient of lift.

    B. Air density.

    C. Blade area.

    D. All of the above.

20. What happens when a helicopter's main rotor blades spin rapidly?

    A. The angle of incidence decreases causing more lift on the retreating blades.

    B. The upper and lower sides of each blade experience a difference in pressure.

    C. Gyroscopic precession acts laterally on the aircraft.

    D. The center of pressure on each blade moves forward, creating a vortex.

21. Newton's Third Law of Motion applies to helicopters because:

    A. The spinning main rotor makes the aircraft try to spin in the opposite direction.

    B. Torque is balanced by the longitudinal drag vector.

    C. A ducted-fan helicopter produces less torque than an un-ducted one.

    D. Rotational relative wind opposes the angular momentum force.

22. When the pilot pushes the cyclic forward:
   A. The main rotor disk tilts forward.
   B. The blades' angle of attack on the rearward section of the tail rotor disk decreases.
   C. The angle of attack of the driven portion of the main rotor disk increases.
   D. All of the above.

23. Multi-engine helicopters have:
   A. A supplementary freewheeling clutch.
   B. A coaxial drive shaft and two transmissions.
   C. A throttle lever for each engine.
   D. All of the above.

24. When the pilot wants the helicopter's nose to move left or right, he or she:
   A. Pushes down on the collective for left motion and pulls up on it to turn right.
   B. Tilts the main rotor disk left or right while keeping the pedals neutral.
   C. Pushes on the left or right pedal while adjusting the cyclic to compensate for greater rotational drag.
   D. Pushes on the corresponding pedal.

25. For helicopters with a main rotor disk that spins counter-clockwise, the _____ airflow speed happens when each blade reaches the _____ position:
   A. median, nine o'clock (left)
   B. minimum, three o'clock (right)
   C. maximum, three o'clock (right)
   D. L/DMAX, six o'clock (aft)

26. On the advancing rotor blade, lift _____ and the blade _____:
   A. increases, angles up near the tip due to greater centripetal force.
   B. increases, moves upward.
   C. transitions outward, experiences stronger lateral torque.
   D. None of the above.

27. The angle between the _____ of a rotor blade and its direction of motion relative to the _____ is the angle of attack (AOA), which is _____ angle.:
   A. mean camber line, air, a constant.
   B. chord line, air, an aerodynamic.
   C. chord line, longitudinal airflow, a variable.
   D. mean camber line, longitudinal airflow, an acute.

28. The angle of incidence is between the _____ line of each blade and the rotor system's _____:

    A. mean chamber, forward-flight relative wind.

    B. mean chamber, rotational relative wind.

    C. chord, angular momentum.

    D. chord, plane of rotation.

29. When a helicopter engine _____, a clutch mechanism called a _____:

    A. fails; governing transmission is disconnected from the engine by the pilot, which allows the main rotor to spin freely.

    B. is shutdown after landing; gearbox controller is disconnected from the engine by the pilot, which allows the main and tail rotors to spin freely.

    C. accelerates too rapidly; terminal speed unit automatically disconnects the engine from the tail rotor, allowing it to spin freely.

    D. fails; freewheeling unit automatically disconnects the engine from the main rotor, allowing it to spin freely.

30. During an autorotation in forward flight, the rotor disk takes in _____ air and the driven, driving, and stall regions of each blade move _____ along its length (span), but only on the _____ side of the disk:

    A. upward flowing, outboard, retreating.

    B. downward flowing, inward, advancing.

    C. upward flowing, inward, retreating.

    D. ambient, outward, advancing.

31. Where there is too much lift, the main rotor blades will:

    A. Torque on the retreating blades.

    B. Twist.

    C. Flap.

    D. Create vortices in the driven region.

32. Centrifugal force _____ spinning helicopter main rotor blades _____.

    A. pushes, inward.

    B. pulls, outward.

    C. angles down, during autorotation.

    D. angles up, during liftoff.

33. If left uncorrected, greater lift produced by the advancing side of the rotor disk compared to the lift created by the disk's retreating side could make the helicopter _____.

    A. fly in a sideslip
    B. vibrate excessively and come apart
    C. torque clockwise
    D. uncontrollable

34. The driven region is _____ the blade tips and normally __ percent of the radius:

    A. nearest, 30
    B. furthest from, 30
    C. mid-span from, 50
    D. nearest, 50

35. The _____ region is normally between a blade's _____ and _____ regions:

    A. stall, driven, high AOA
    B. stall, driving, low AOA
    C. driven, high AOA, stall
    D. driving, stall, driven

36. Because of gyroscopic precession, if a wind gust applies a downward force on the left side of a helicopter's main rotor disk as it spins clockwise (as viewed from above), the movement response occurs at the __ o'clock position:

    A. 9
    B. 6
    C. 12
    D. 3

37. Helicopters experience effective translational lift while transitioning to forward flight at approximately __ to __ knots:

    A. 20, 28
    B. 10, 20
    C. 16, 24
    D. 12, 24

38. Maximum ground effect occurs during a hover up to a height equal to ___ percent of the main rotor's diameter:

    A. 50

    B. 100

    C. 150

    D. None of the above

39. A pilot can worsen a helicopter's pendular action by:

    A. Applying too much angle of incidence.

    B. Over-controlling the aircraft.

    C. Moving the cyclic left while pushing on the right pedal.

    D. Moving the cyclic left while pulling up on the collective.

40. The phenomenon of a helicopter sinking into its own downwash is called:

    A. L/Wmin (minimum lift-to-weight ratio).

    B. An airfoil stall.

    C. Vortex torque state.

    D. Settling with power.

Army Aviation Information Practice Test Answers Key

1. B		21. A	
2. C		22. A	
3. B		23. C	
4. A		24. D	
5. D		25. C	
6. A		26. B	
7. B		27. B	
8. C		28. D	
9. C		29. D	
10. D		30. A	
11. B		31. C	
12. A		32. B	
13. C		33. D	
14. D		34. A	
15. D		35. D	
16. D		36. C	
17. A		37. C	
18. C		38. B	
19. D		39. B	
20. B		40. D	

Chapter Four: Spatial Apperception

The Spatial Apperception section is simple, but deceiving. The best method to beating this section is to use a strategy for each and every question. Missed questions are 99% attributable to the test-taker looking at the question, abandoning their strategy because an answer "just looks right" at first glance. You will have 10 minutes to answer 25 questions, which is actually ample time once you get familiarized with the format.

First, let's review how the test is formatted. On the following page, you'll see there is an image of a horizon, typically with both water and land or some other distinguishable features to use as references. Imagine this is the view from the cockpit of an aircraft. Below this image, you will have 5 multiple choice options. Each option, A through E, shows the aircraft relative to the ground. Your task is to determine which aircraft represents the view from the cockpit.

The absolutely best strategy for this section is to employ a process of elimination and to follow that process strictly for each question. In each answer choice, the aircraft might be diving or climbing or flying level, banking left or right at various degrees or not banking at all, and traveling any direction (inbound, outbound, etc). It is best to start with the easiest and most obvious identifier, banking. For example, if you see that the image from the cockpit is flat and level, you can immediately remove any answer choice with any amount of bank either left or right which is represented by the horizon being tilted at an angle. If the horizon tilts UP to the right, the aircraft is banking right. If the horizon tilts UP to the left, the aircraft is banking left.

Next in the process of elimination, determine if the view from the cockpit is climbing or diving or level. This can be a little trickier because the differences are much more subtle and sometimes hard to distinguish. The best method is to find the vertical center-point of the view from the aircraft. If the horizon is ABOVE the centerpoint, the aircraft is diving. If it is BELOW the centerpoint, the aircraft is climbing. Remember, although it is more subtle than determining whether the aircraft is banking, this section is not intended to be devious such that you will have 5 answer choices of all aircraft in a dive but slightly more or less.

Finally, determine the orientation of the aircraft. For example, if the view from the cockpit shows water from edge to edge, you are obviously flying out to sea. So if there are answer choices showing the aircraft flying inbound to land or flying parallel to the coast, those are obviously incorrect.

This process of elimination can of course be modified for each test-taker. Some people find the orientation of the aircraft the most obvious and easy, so choose to start their process of elimination with that. Often, it is the diving and climbing that unnerves test-takers simply because they over-think it.

The following are some views from the aircraft with the attributable features:

Slight dive, no bank, & flying inbound to land (the "Land" is the dark area, the "water" is indicated with the little lines to represent waves). Notice the horizon is slightly above the center-point.

Climbing, no bank, & flying out to sea (note the horizon below the center-point)

Climbing, banking left, flying parallel to land (remember, the horizon slopes UP to the left, so the aircraft is banking left. The horizon is slightly below the center-point, so must be climbing).

Remember that with climbing and diving, the differences can be quite subtle. Do not overthink this! The answer choices are often quite different and by process of elimination, you will likely never encounter any problem where you have 2 or more answer choices that are too similar. Use the process of elimination and the correct answer will reveal itself.

Next, views of the aircraft with attributable features:

❖ Aircraft flying flat and level, no bank

❖ Aircraft flying at slight climb, banking left

❖ Aircraft diving, no bank (possibly slight bank, but depends on viewpoint)

❖ Aircraft climbing, banking left

Finally, let's look at an example problem and work through it step-by-step:

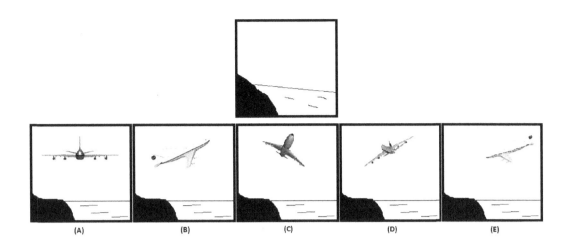

Remember, you can choose your own order of elimination, just start with whatever attribute is easiest for you to identify. In this case, let's start with direction of travel. In the view from the aircraft, it is obviously flying along the coastline. Therefore, answer choices B and E are immediately out because B is flying out to sea and E is flying inbound to land.

Next, still in terms of direction of travel, the land is on the left side of the image. Because of that, we know answer choice C must be incorrect as the view from the cockpit would have the land on the right side.

We are now down to only choices A and D remaining. As you can see from the view from the aircraft, the horizon is tilted, so we know the aircraft is banking. Without even worrying about what direction it is banking (FYI: it is banking left b/c the horizon slopes UP to the left), we know that answer choice A is incorrect because that aircraft is flat and level.

The only possible answer choice is D. You will note that we did not even get to whether the aircraft was in a climb or dive. In this case, the aircraft in answer choice D appears to be in a very slight climb. This helps illustrate the subtleness of the viewpoint from the cockpit. As you can see, the horizon is slightly below the center-point, although the land does climb slightly higher which can throw some people off. Typically, it's best to look at the water for a reference point since there are no variations in altitude.

Let's get started with the practice test. You will encounter 25 questions on the real test, for which you have 10 minutes to answer. That seems like a short time, but after the first couple of practice questions and get the feel for it, most people notice they can answer the questions easily in under 15-20 seconds. Again, once you get the hang of this section, move on to something else.

Spatial Apperception Practice Test

1.

2.

3.

(A)   (B)   (C)   (D)   (E)

4.

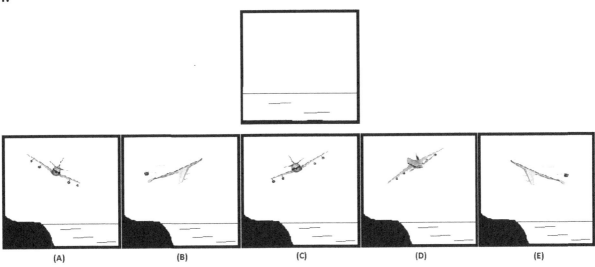

(A)   (B)   (C)   (D)   (E)

49

5.

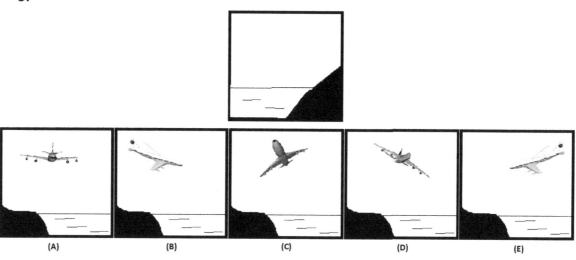

(A)   (B)   (C)   (D)   (E)

6.

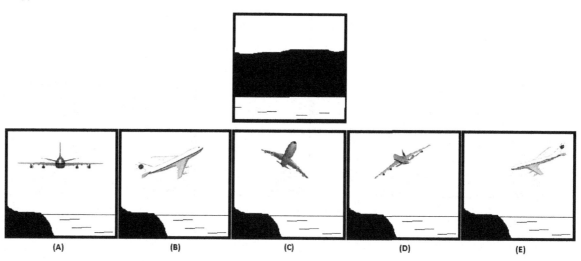

(A)   (B)   (C)   (D)   (E)

7.

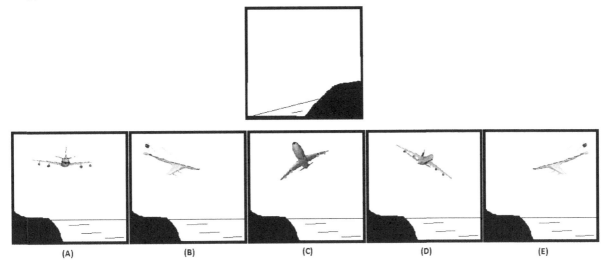

(A)   (B)   (C)   (D)   (E)

8.

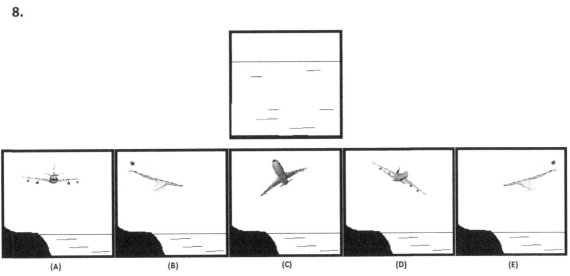

(A)   (B)   (C)   (D)   (E)

9.

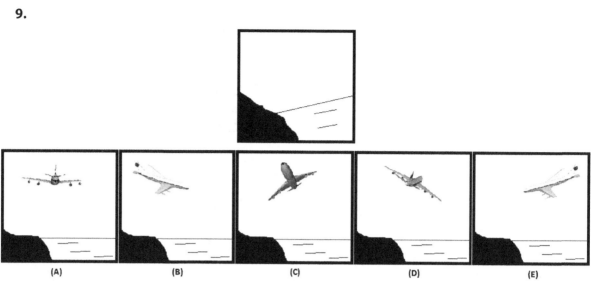

(A)   (B)   (C)   (D)   (E)

10.

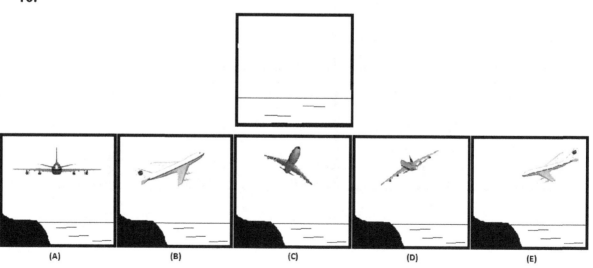

(A)   (B)   (C)   (D)   (E)

11.

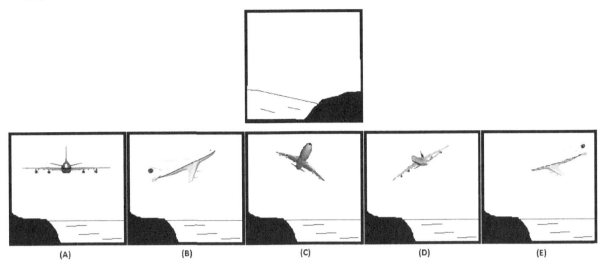

(A)　　　(B)　　　(C)　　　(D)　　　(E)

12.

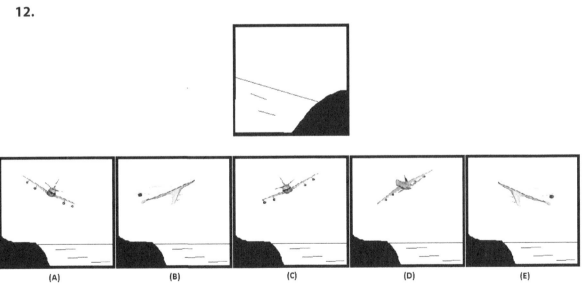

(A)　　　(B)　　　(C)　　　(D)　　　(E)

13.

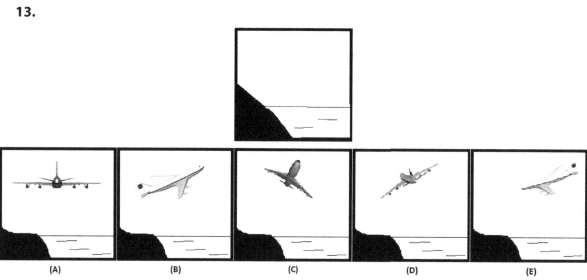

(A) (B) (C) (D) (E)

14.

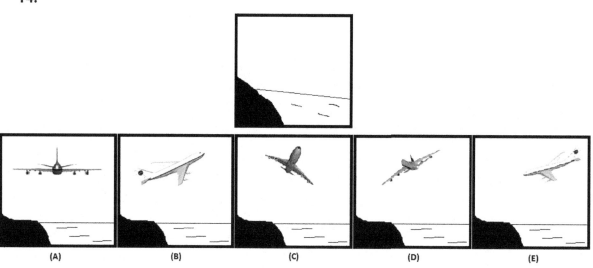

(A) (B) (C) (D) (E)

15.

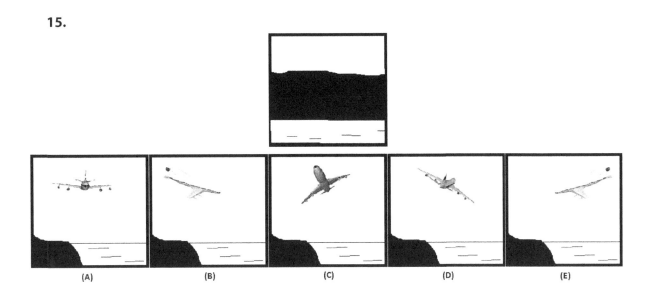

(A)   (B)   (C)   (D)   (E)

Spatial Apperception Practice Test Answer Key

1. D
2. C
3. E
4. B
5. A
6. E
7. C
8. B
9. D
10. B
11. C
12. A
13. A
14. D
15. E

Chapter Five: Reading Comprehension

The Reading Comprehension test measures your ability to understand, analyze, and evaluate written passages. You will be given 20 questions with a 30 minute time limit. The questions will generally be formatted such that you are presented a short passage and asked to find the answer choice that could have been inferred from only the information presented in the passage. The trick of this section is that many of the answer choices might be "true" or "feasible", but you will have to select the "best" answer.

We will cover the methods to best decipher and dissect the necessary information from a passage so that you can more quickly and accurately find the correct answer. After that, there are practice questions to help reinforce the review section so that the Reading Comprehension exam becomes relatively easy for you.

Reading

The Reading section of the exam will assess your ability to summarize, interpret, and draw conclusions about both non-fiction and fiction passages. You'll be asked questions about:

- ❖ the main idea of a passage
- ❖ the role of supporting details in the passage
- ❖ adding supporting details to the passage
- ❖ the structure of the passage
- ❖ the author's purpose
- ❖ logical inferences that can be drawn from the passage
- ❖ comparing passages
- ❖ understanding vocabulary and figurative language

The SIFT Reading section will require you to read both non-fiction and fiction passages and then answer questions about them. These questions will fall into three main categories:

- ❖ **About the Author:** The question will ask about the author's attitude, thoughts, and opinions. When encountering a question asking specifically about the author, pay attention to context clues in the article. The answer may not be explicitly stated but instead conveyed in the overall message.
- ❖ **Passage Facts:** You must distinguish between facts and opinions presented in the passage. You may also be asked to identify specific information supplied by the author of the passage.
- ❖ **Additional Information:** These questions will have you look at what kind of information could be added to or was missing from the passage. They may also ask in what direction the passage was going. Questions may ask what statement could be added to strengthen the author's statement, or weaken it; they may also provide a fill-in-the-blank option to include a statement that is missing from, but fits with the rest of, the passage.

The Reading section will also include informational source comprehension questions. These questions don't refer back to a text passage; instead, they will ask you to interpret an informational source like a nutrition label, map, or thermometer. (These questions are covered in the section below titled "Informational Source Comprehension.")

Strategies

Despite the different types of questions you will face, there are some strategies for Reading Comprehension which apply across the board:

❖ Read the answer choices first, then read the passage. This will save you time, as you will know what to look out for as you read.

❖ Use the process of elimination. Some answer choices are obviously incorrect and are relatively easy to detect. After reading the passage, eliminate those blatantly incorrect answer choices; this increases your chance of finding the correct answer much more quickly.

❖ Avoid negative statements. Generally, test-makers will not make negative statements about anyone or anything. Statements will be either neutral or positive, so if it seems like an answer choice has a negative connotation, it is very likely that the answer is intentionally false.

The Main Idea

The main idea of a text is the purpose behind why a writer would choose to write a book, article, story, etc. Being able to find and understand the main idea is a critical skill necessary to comprehend and appreciate what you're reading.

Consider a political election. A candidate is running for office and plans to deliver a speech asserting her position on tax reform. The **topic** of the speech—tax reform—is clear to voters, and probably of interest to many. However, imagine that the candidate believes that taxes should be lowered. She is likely to assert this argument in her speech, supporting it with examples proving why lowering taxes would benefit the public and how it could be accomplished. While the topic of the speech would be tax reform, the benefit of lowering taxes would be the **main idea**. Other candidates may have different perspectives on the topic; they may believe that higher taxes are necessary, or that current taxes are adequate. It is likely that their speeches, while on the same topic of tax reform, would have different main ideas: different arguments likewise supported by different examples. Determining what a speaker, writer, or text is asserting about a specific issue will reveal the main idea.

One more quick note: the exam may also ask about a passage's **theme**, which is similar to but distinct from its topic. While a topic is usually a specific *person, place, thing,* or *issue,* the theme is an *idea* or *concept* that the author refers back to frequently. Examples of common themes include ideas like the importance of family, the dangers of technology, and the beauty of nature.

There will be many questions on the exam that require you to differentiate between the topic, theme, and main idea of a passage. Let's look at an example passage to see how you would answer these questions.

"Babe Didrikson Zaharias, one of the most decorated female athletes of the twentieth century, is an inspiration for everyone. Born in 1911 in Beaumont, Texas, Zaharias lived in a time when women were considered second-class to men, but she never let that stop her from becoming a champion. Babe was one of seven children in a poor immigrant family, and was competitive from an early age. As a child she excelled at most things she tried, especially sports, which continued into high school and beyond. After high school, Babe played amateur basketball for two years, and soon after began training in track and field. Despite the fact that women were only allowed to enter in three events, Babe represented the United States in the 1932 Los Angeles Olympics, and won two gold medals and one silver for track and field events.

"In the early 1930s, Babe began playing golf which earned her a legacy. The first tournament she entered was a men's only tournament, however she did not make the cut to play. Playing golf as an amateur was the only option for a woman at this time, since there was no professional women's league. Babe played as an amateur for a little over a decade, until she turned pro in 1947 for the Ladies Professional Golf Association (LPGA) of which she was a founding member. During her career as a golfer, Babe won eighty-two tournaments, amateur and professional, including the U.S. Women's Open, All-American Open, and British Women's Open Golf Tournament. In 1953, Babe was diagnosed with cancer, but fourteen weeks later, she played in a tournament. That year she won her third U.S. Women's Open. However by 1955, she didn't have the physicality to compete anymore, and she died of the disease in 1956."

The topic of this paragraph is obviously Babe Zaharias—the whole passage describes events from her life. Determining the main idea, however, requires a little more analysis. The passage describes Babe Zaharias' life, but the main idea of the paragraph is what it says about her life. To figure out the main idea, consider what the writer is saying about Babe Zaharias. The writer is saying that she's someone to admire—that's the main idea and what unites all the information in the paragraph. Lastly, what might the theme of the passage be? The writer refers to several broad concepts, including never giving up and overcoming the odds, both of which could be themes for the passage. Two major indicators of the main idea of a paragraph or passage follow below:

❖ It is a general idea; it applies to all the more specific ideas in the passage. Every other sentence in a paragraph should be able to relate in some way to the main idea.

❖ It asserts a specific viewpoint that the author supports with facts, opinions, or other details. In other words, the main idea takes a stand.

EXAMPLE

From so far away it's easy to imagine the surface of our solar system's planets as enigmas—how could we ever know what those far-flung planets really look like? It turns out, however, that scientists have a number of tools at their disposal that allow them to paint detailed pictures of many planets' surfaces. The topography of Venus, for example, has been explored by several space probes, including the Russian Venera landers and NASA's Magellan orbiter. These craft used imaging and radar to map the surface of the planet, identifying a whole host of features including volcanoes, craters, and a complex system of channels. Mars has similarly been mapped by space probes, including the famous Mars Rovers, which are automated vehicles that actually landed on the surface of Mars. These rovers have been used by NASA and other space agencies to study the geology, climate, and possible biology of the planet.

In addition these long-range probes, NASA has also used its series of orbiting telescopes to study distant planets. These four massively powerful telescopes include the famous Hubble Space Telescope as well as the Compton Gamma Ray Observatory, Chandra X-Ray Observatory, and the Spitzer Space Telescope. Scientists can use these telescopes to examine planets using not only visible light but also infrared and near-infrared light, ultraviolet light, x-rays and gamma rays.

Powerful telescopes aren't just found in space: NASA makes use of Earth-bound telescopes as well. Scientists at the National Radio Astronomy Observatory in Charlottesville, VA, have spent decades using radio imaging to build an incredibly detailed portrait of Venus' surface. In fact, Earth-bound telescopes offer a distinct advantage over orbiting telescopes because they allow scientists to capture data from a fixed point, which in turn allows them to effectively compare data collected over long period of time.

Which of the following sentences best describes the main of the passage?
- **A.** It's impossible to know what the surfaces of other planets are really like.
- **B.** Telescopes are an important tool for scientists studying planets in our solar system.
- **C.** Venus' surface has many of the same features as the Earth's, including volcanoes, craters, and channels.
- **D.** Scientists use a variety of advanced technologies to study the surface of the planets in our solar system.

Answer: Answer A) can be eliminated because it directly contradicts the rest of the passage, which goes into detail about how scientists have learned about the surfaces of other planets. Answers B) and C) can also be eliminated because they offer only specific details from the passage—while both choices contain details from the passage, neither is general enough to encompass the passage as a whole. Only answer D) provides an assertion that is both backed up by the passage's content and general enough to cover the entire passage.

Topic and Summary Sentences

The main idea of a paragraph usually appears within the topic sentence. The **topic sentence** introduces the main idea to readers; it indicates not only the topic of a passage, but also the writer's perspective on the topic.

Notice, for example, how the first sentence in the example paragraph about Babe Zaharias states the main idea: Babe Didrikson Zaharias, one of the most decorated female athletes of the twentieth century, is an inspiration for everyone.

Even though paragraphs generally begin with topic sentences due to their introductory nature, on occasion writers build up to the topic sentence by using supporting details in order to generate interest or build an argument. Be alert for paragraphs when writers do not include a clear topic sentence at all; even without a clear topic sentence, a paragraph will still have a main idea. You may also see a **summary sentence** at the end of a passage. As its name suggests, this sentence sums up the passage, often by restating the main idea and the author's key evidence supporting it.

EXAMPLE

In the following paragraph, what are the topic and summary sentences?

The Constitution of the United States establishes a series of limits to rein in centralized power. Separation of powers distributes federal authority among three competing branches: the executive, the legislative, and the judicial. Checks and balances allow the branches to check the usurpation of power by any one branch. States' rights are protected under the Constitution from too much encroachment by the federal government. Enumeration of powers names the specific and few powers the federal government has. These four restrictions have helped sustain the American republic for over two centuries.

Answer: The topic sentence is the first sentence in the paragraph. It introduces the topic of discussion, in this case the constitutional limits aimed at resisting centralized power. The summary sentence is the last sentence in the paragraph. It sums up the information that was just presented: here, that constitutional limits have helped sustain the United States of America for over two hundred years.

Implied Main Idea

A paragraph without a clear topic sentence still has a main idea; rather than clearly stated, it is implied. Determining the **implied main idea** requires some detective work: you will need to look at the author's word choice and tone in addition to the content of the passage to find his or her main idea.

EXAMPLES

One of my summer reading books was *Mockingjay*. Though it's several hundred pages long, I read it in just a few days. I was captivated by the adventures of the main character and the complicated plot of the book. However, I felt like the ending didn't reflect the excitement of the story. Given what a powerful personality the main character has, I felt like the ending didn't do her justice.

1. Even without a clear topic sentence, this paragraph has a main idea. What is the writer's perspective on the book; what is the writer saying about it?
    A. *Mockingjay* is a terrific novel.
    B. *Mockingjay* is disappointing.
    C. *Mockingjay* is full of suspense.
    D. *Mockingjay* is a lousy novel.

Answer: The correct answer is B): the novel is disappointing. The process of elimination will reveal the correct answer if that is not immediately clear. While that the paragraph begins with positive commentary on the book—I was captivated by the adventures of the main character and the complicated plot of the book—this positive idea is followed by the contradictory transition word however. A) cannot be the correct answer because the author concludes that the novel was poor. Likewise, D) cannot be correct because it does not encompass all the ideas in the paragraph; despite the negative conclusion, the author enjoyed most of the book. The main idea should be able to encompass all of the thoughts in a paragraph; choice D) does not apply to the beginning of this paragraph. Finally, choice C) is too specific; it could only apply to the brief description of the plot and adventures of the main character. That leaves choice B) as the best option. The author initially enjoyed the book, but was disappointed by the ending, which seemed unworthy of the exciting plot and character.

Fortunately, none of Alyssa's coworkers has ever seen inside the large filing drawer in her desk. Disguised by the meticulous neatness of the rest of her workspace, there was no sign of the chaos beneath. To even open it, she had to struggle for several minutes with the enormous pile of junk jamming the drawer, until it would suddenly give way, and papers, folders, and candy wrappers spilled out of the top and onto the floor. It was an organizational nightmare, with torn notes and spreadsheets haphazardly thrown on top of each other, and melted candy smeared across pages. She was worried the odor would soon permeate to her coworker's desks, revealing to them her secret.

2. Which sentence best describes the main idea of the paragraph above?
    A. Alyssa wishes she could move to a new desk.
    B. Alyssa wishes she had her own office.
    C. Alyssa is glad none of her coworkers know about her messy drawer.
    D. Alyssa is sad because she doesn't have any coworkers.

Clearly, Alyssa has a messy drawer, and C) is the right answer. The paragraph begins by indicating her gratitude that her coworkers do not know about her drawer (*Fortunately, none of Alyssa's coworkers has ever seen inside the large filing drawer in her desk.*) Plus, notice how the drawer is described: *it was an organizational nightmare*, and it apparently doesn't even function properly: *to even open the drawer, she had to struggle for several minutes*. The writer reveals that it has an odor, with *melted candy* inside. Alyssa is clearly ashamed of her drawer and fearful of being judged by her coworkers for it.

Supporting Details

Supporting details provide more support for the author's main idea. For instance, in the Babe Zaharias example above, the writer makes the general assertion that "Babe Didrikson Zaharias, one of the most decorated female athletes of the twentieth century, is an inspiration for everyone." The rest of the paragraph provides supporting details with facts showing why Babe Zaharias is an inspiration: the struggles she faced as a female athlete, and the specific years she competed in the Olympics and in golf.

Writers often provide clues that can help you identify supporting details. Be alert for **signal words,** which can be helpful in identifying supporting details. Signal words can also help you rule out sentences that are not the main idea or topic sentence: if a sentence begins with one of these phrases, it will likely be too specific to be a main idea.

Questions on the SIFT will ask you to do two things with supporting details: you will need to find details that support a particular idea and also explain why a particular detail was included in the passage. In order to answer these questions, you need to have a solid understanding of the passage's main idea. With this knowledge, you can determine how a supporting detail fits in with the larger structure of the passage.

EXAMPLES

From so far away it's easy to imagine the surface of our solar system's planets as enigmas—how could we ever know what those far-flung planets really look like? It turns out, however, that scientists have a number of tools at their disposal that allow them to paint detailed pictures of many planets' surfaces. The topography of Venus, for example, has been explored by several space probes, including the Russian *Venera* landers and NASA's *Magellan* orbiter. These craft used imaging and radar to map the surface of the planet, identifying a whole host of features including volcanoes, craters, and a complex system of channels. Mars has similarly been mapped by space probes, including the famous Mars Rovers, which are automated vehicles that actually landed on the surface of Mars. These rovers have been used by NASA and other space agencies to study the geology, climate, and possible biology of the planet.

In addition these long-range probes, NASA has also used its series of orbiting telescopes to study distant planets. These four massively powerful telescopes include the famous Hubble Space Telescope as well as the Compton Gamma Ray Observatory, Chandra X-Ray Observatory, and the Spitzer Space Telescope. Scientists can use these telescopes to examine planets using not only visible light but also infrared and near-infrared light, ultraviolet light, x-rays and gamma rays.

Powerful telescopes aren't just found in space: NASA makes use of Earth-bound telescopes as well. Scientists at the National Radio Astronomy Observatory in Charlottesville, VA, have spent decades using radio imaging to build an incredibly detailed portrait of Venus' surface. In fact, Earth-bound telescopes offer a distinct advantage over orbiting telescopes because they allow scientists to capture data from a fixed point, which in turn allows them to effectively compare data collected over long period of time.

1. Which sentence from the text best helps develop the idea that scientists make use of many different technologies to study the surfaces of other planets?
    A. These rovers have been used by NASA and other space agencies to study the geology, climate, and possible biology of the planet.
    B. From so far away it's easy to imagine the surface of our solar system's planets as enigmas—how could we ever know what those far-flung planets really look like?
    C. In addition these long-range probes, NASA has also used its series of orbiting telescopes to study distant planets.
    D. These craft used imaging and radar to map the surface of the planet, identifying a whole host of features including volcanoes, craters, and a complex system of channels.

Answer: You're looking for detail from the passage that supports the main idea—scientists make use of many different technologies to study the surfaces of other planets. Answer A) includes a specific detail about rovers, but does not offer any details that support the idea of multiple technologies being used. Similarly, answer D) provides another specific detail about space probes. Answer B) doesn't provide any supporting details; it simply introduces the topic of the passage. Only answer C) provides a detail that directly supports the author's assertion that scientists use multiple technologies to study the planets.

2. If true, which detail could be added to the passage above to support the author's argument that scientists use many different technologies to study the surface of planets?
    A. Because the Earth's atmosphere blocks x-rays, gamma rays, and infrared radiation, NASA needed to put telescopes in orbit above the atmosphere.

B. In 2015, NASA released a map of Venus which was created by compiling images from orbiting telescopes and long-range space probes.

C. NASA is currently using the *Curiosity* and *Opportunity* rovers to look for signs of ancient life on Mars.

D. NASA has spent over $2.5 billion to build, launch, and repair the Hubble Space Telescope.

Answer: You can eliminate answers C) and D) because they don't address the topic of studying the surface of planets. Answer A) can also be eliminated because it only addresses a single technology. Only choice B) provides would add support to the author's claim about the importance of using multiple technologies.

3. The author likely included the detail Earth-bound telescopes offer a distinct advantage over orbiting telescopes because they allow scientists to capture data from a fixed point in order to:

   A. Explain why it has taken scientists so long to map the surface of Venus.

   B. Suggest that Earth-bound telescopes are the most important equipment used by NASA scientists.

   C. Prove that orbiting telescopes will soon be replaced by Earth-bound telescopes.

   D. Demonstrate why NASA scientists rely on my different types of scientific equipment.

Answer: Only answer D) directs directly to the author's main argument. The author doesn't mention how long it has taken to map the surface of Venus (answer A), nor does he say that one technology is more important than the others (answer B). And while this detail does highlight the advantages of using Earth-bound telescopes, the author's argument is that many technologies are being used at the same time, so there's no reason to think that orbiting telescopes will be replaced (answer C).

Text Structure

Authors can structure passages in a number of different ways. These distinct organizational patterns, referred to as **text structure**, use the logical relationships between ideas to improve the readability and coherence of a text. The most common ways passages are organized include:

❖ **problem-solution**: the author presents a problem and then discusses a solution

❖ **comparison-contrast**: the author presents two situations and then discusses the similarities and differences

❖ **cause-effect**: the author presents an action and then discusses the resulting effects

❖ **descriptive**: an idea, object, person, or other item is described in detail

EXAMPLE

The issue of public transportation has begun to haunt the fast-growing cities of the southern United States. Unlike their northern counterparts, cities like Atlanta, Dallas, and Houston have long promoted growth out and not up—these are cities full of sprawling suburbs and single-family homes, not densely concentrated skyscrapers and apartments. What to do then, when all those suburbanites need to get into the central business districts for work? For a long time it seemed highways were the answer: twenty-lane wide expanses of concrete that would allow commuters to move from home to work and back again. But these modern miracles have become time-sucking, pollution spewing nightmares. They may not like it, but it's time for these cities to turn toward public transport like trains and buses if they want their cities to remain livable.

The organization of this passage can best be described as:

A. a comparison of two similar ideas

B. a description of a place

C. a discussion of several effects all related to the same cause

D. a discussion of a problem followed by the suggestion of a solution

Answer: You can exclude answer choice C) because the author provides no root cause or a list of effects. From there this question gets tricky, because the passage contains structures similar to those described above. For example, it compares two things (cities in the North and South) and describes a place (a sprawling city). However, if you look at the overall organization of the passage, you can see that it starts by presenting a problem (transportation) and then presents a solution (trains and buses), making answer D) the only choice that encompasses the entire passage.

The Author's Purpose

Whenever an author writes a text, she always has a purpose, whether that's to entertain, inform, explain, or persuade. A short story, for example, is meant to entertain, while an online news article would be designed to inform the public about a current event.

Each of these different types of writing has a specific name. On the exam, you will be asked to identify which of these categories a passage fits into:

- ❖ **Narrative writing** tells a story. (novel, short story, play)
- ❖ **Expository writing** informs people. (newspaper and magazine articles)
- ❖ **Technical writing** explains something. (product manual, directions)
- ❖ **Persuasive writing** tries to convince the reader of something. (opinion column on a blog)

You may also be asked about primary and secondary sources. These terms describe not the writing itself but the author's relationship to what's being written about. A **primary source** is an unaltered piece of writing that was composed during the time when the events being described took place; these texts are often written by the people involved. A **secondary source** might address the same topic but provides extra commentary or analysis. These texts can be written by people not directly involved in the events. For example, a book written by a political candidate to inform people about his or her stand on an issue is a primary source; an online article written by a journalist analyzing how that position will affect the election is a secondary source.

EXAMPLE

Elizabeth closed her eyes and braced herself on the armrests that divided her from her fellow passengers. Take-off was always the worst part for her. The revving of the engines, the way her stomach dropped as the plane lurched upward: it made her feel sick. Then, she had to watch the world fade away beneath her, getting smaller and smaller until it was just her and the clouds hurtling through the sky. Sometimes (but only sometimes) it just had to be endured, though. She focused on the thought of her sister's smiling face and her new baby nephew as the plane slowly pulled onto the runway.

The passage above is reflective of which type of writing?
- **A.** Narrative
- **B.** Expository
- **C.** Technical
- **D.** Persuasive

Answer: The passage is telling a story—we meet Elizabeth and learn about her fear of flying—so it's a narrative text. There is no factual information presented or explained, nor is the author trying to persuade the reader.

Facts vs. Opinions

On the exam Reading passages you might be asked to identify a statement in a passage as either a fact or an opinion, so you'll need to know the difference between the two. A **fact** is a statement or thought that can be proven to be true. The statement *Wednesday comes after Tuesday* is a fact—you can point to a calendar to prove it. In contrast, an **opinion** is an assumption that is not based in fact and cannot be proven to be true. The assertion that *television is more entertaining than feature films* is an opinion—people will disagree on this, and there's no reference you can use to prove or disprove it.

EXAMPLE

Exercise is critical for healthy development in children. Today, there is an epidemic of unhealthy children in the United States who will face health problems in adulthood due to poor diet and lack of exercise as children. This is a problem for all Americans, especially with the rising cost of healthcare.

It is vital that school systems and parents encourage their children to engage in a minimum of thirty minutes of cardiovascular exercise each day, mildly increasing their heart rate for a sustained period. This is proven to decrease the likelihood of developmental diabetes, obesity, and a multitude of other health problems. Also, children need a proper diet rich in fruits and vegetables so that they can grow and develop physically, as well as learn healthy eating habits early on.

Which of the following is a fact in the passage, not an opinion?
- **A.** Fruits and vegetables are the best way to help children be healthy.
- **B.** Children today are lazier than they were in previous generations.
- **C.** The risk of diabetes in children is reduced by physical activity.
- **D.** Children should engage in thirty minutes of exercise a day.

Answer: Choice B) can be discarded immediately because it is negative and is not discussed anywhere in the passage. Answers A) and D) are both opinions—the author is promoting exercise, fruits, and vegetables as a way to make children healthy. (Notice that these incorrect answers contain words that hint at being an opinion such as *best*, *should*, or other comparisons.) Answer B), on the other hand, is a simple fact stated by the author; it's introduced by the word *proven* to indicate that you don't need to just take the author's word for it.

Drawing Conclusions

In addition to understanding the main idea and factual content of a passage, you'll also be asked to take your analysis one step further and anticipate what other information could logically be added to the passage. In a non-fiction passage, for example, you might be asked which statement the author of the passage would agree with. In an excerpt from a fictional work, you might be asked to anticipate what the character would do next.

To answer these questions, you need to have a solid understanding of the topic, theme, and main idea of the passage; armed with this information, you can figure out which of the answer choices best fits within those criteria (or alternatively, which ones do not). For example, if the author of the passage is advocating for safer working conditions in textile factories, any supporting details that would be added to the passage should support that idea. You might add sentences that contain information about the number of accidents that occur in textile factories or that outline a new plan for fire safety.

EXAMPLE

Today, there is an epidemic of unhealthy children in the United States who will face health problems in adulthood due to poor diet and lack of exercise during their childhood. This is a problem for all Americans, as adults with chronic health issues are adding to the rising cost of healthcare. A child who grows up living an unhealthy lifestyle is likely to become an adult who does the same.

Because exercise is critical for healthy development in children, it is vital that school systems and parents encourage their children to engage in a minimum of thirty minutes of cardiovascular exercise each day. Even this small amount of exercise has been proven to decrease the likelihood that young people will develop diabetes, obesity, and other health issues as adults. In addition to exercise, children need a proper diet rich in fruits and vegetables so that they can grow and develop physically. Starting a good diet early also teaches children healthy eating habits they will carry into adulthood.

1. The author of this passage would most likely agree with which statement?
    A. Parents are solely responsible for the health of their children.
    B. Children who do not want to exercise should not be made to.
    C. Improved childhood nutrition will help lower the amount Americans spend on healthcare.
    D. It's not important to teach children healthy eating habits because they will learn them as adults.

Answer: The author would most likely support answer C): he mentions in the first paragraph that unhealthy habits are adding to the rising cost of healthcare. The main idea of the passage is that nutrition and exercise are important for children, so answer B) doesn't make sense—the author would likely support measures to encourage children to exercise. Answers A) and D) can also be eliminated because they are directly contradicted in the text. The author specifically mentions the role of schools systems, so he doesn't believe parents are solely responsible for their children's health. He also specifically states that children who grow up with unhealthy habit will become adults with unhealthy habits, which contradicts D).

Elizabeth closed her eyes and braced herself on the armrests that divided her from her fellow passengers. Take-off was always the worst part for her. The revving of the engines, the way her stomach dropped as the plane lurched upward: it made her feel sick. Then, she had to watch the world fade away beneath her, getting smaller and smaller until it was just her and the clouds hurtling through the sky. Sometimes (but only sometimes) it just had to be endured, though. She focused on the thought of her sister's smiling face and her new baby nephew as the plane slowly pulled onto the runway.

2. Which of the following is Elizabeth least likely to do in the future?
    A. Take a flight to her brother's wedding.
    B. Apply for a job as a flight attendant.
    C. Never board an airplane again.
    D. Get sick on an airplane.

Answer: It's clear from the passage that Elizabeth hates flying, but it willing to endure it for the sake of visiting her family. Thus, it seems likely that she would be willing to get on a plane for her brother's wedding, making A) and C) incorrect answers. The passage also explicitly tells us that she feels sick on planes, so D) is likely to happen. We can infer, though, that she would not enjoy being on an airplane for work, so she's very unlikely to apply for a job as a flight attendant, which is choice B).

Meaning of Words and Phrases

On the Reading section you may also be asked to provide definitions or intended meanings for words within passages. You may have never encountered some of these words before the test, but there are tricks you can use to figure out what they mean.

Context Clues

The most fundamental vocabulary skill is using the context in which a word is used to determine its meaning. Your ability to observe sentences closely is extremely useful when it comes to understanding new vocabulary words.

There are two types of context that can help you understand the meaning of unfamiliar words: situational context and sentence context. Regardless of which context is present, these types of questions are not really testing your knowledge of vocabulary; rather, they test your ability to comprehend the meaning of a word through its usage.

Situational context is context that is presented by the setting or circumstances in which a word or phrase occurs. **Sentence context** occurs within the specific sentence that contains the vocabulary word. To figure out words using sentence context clues, you should first determine the most important words in the sentence.

There are four types of clues that can help you understand context, and therefore the meaning of a word:

- ❖ **Restatement** clues occur when the definition of the word is clearly stated in the sentence.
- ❖ **Positive/negative clues** can tell you whether a word has a positive or negative meaning.
- ❖ **Contrast clues** include the opposite meaning of a word. Words like *but, on the other hand*, and *however* are tip-offs that a sentence contains a contrast clue.
- ❖ **Specific detail clues** provide a precise detail that can help you understand the meaning of the word.

It is important to remember that more than one of these clues can be present in the same sentence. The more there are, the easier it will be to determine the meaning of the word. For example, the following sentence uses both restatement and positive/negative clues: *Janet suddenly found herself destitute, so poor she could barely afford to eat.* The second part of the sentence clearly indicates that *destitute* is a negative word. It also restates the meaning: very poor.

EXAMPLES

1. I had a hard time reading her *illegible* handwriting.
    - **A.** neat
    - **B.** unsafe
    - **C.** sloppy
    - **D.** educated

Answer: Already, you know that this sentence is discussing something that is hard to read. Look at the word that *illegible* is describing: handwriting. Based on context clues, you can tell that *illegible* means that her handwriting is hard to read.

Next, look at the answer choices. Choice A), *neat,* is obviously a wrong answer because neat handwriting would not be difficult to read. Choices B) and D), *unsafe* and *educated,* don't make sense. Therefore, choice C), *sloppy,* is the best answer.

2. The dog was *dauntless* in the face of danger, braving the fire to save the girl trapped inside the building.
    A. difficult
    B. fearless
    C. imaginative
    D. startled

Answer: Demonstrating bravery in the face of danger would be B) *fearless.* In this case, the restatement clue (*braving the fire*) tells you exactly what the word means.

3. Beth did not spend any time preparing for the test, but Tyrone kept a *rigorous* study schedule.
    A. strict
    B. loose
    C. boring
    D. strange

Answer: In this case, the contrast word *but* tells us that Tyrone studied in a different way than Beth, which means it's a contrast clue. If Beth did not study hard, then Tyrone did. The best answer, therefore, is choice A).

Analyzing Words

As you no doubt know, determining the meaning of a word can be more complicated than just looking in a dictionary. A word might have more than one **denotation**, or definition; which one the author intends can only be judged by looking at the surrounding text. For example, the word *quack* can refer to the sound a duck makes, or to a person who publicly pretends to have a qualification which he or she does not actually possess.

A word may also have different **connotations**, which are the implied meanings and emotion a word evokes in the reader. For example, a cubicle is a simply a walled desk in an office, but for many the word implies a constrictive, uninspiring workplace. Connotations can vary greatly between cultures and even between individuals.

Lastly, authors might make use of **figurative language**, which is the use of a word to imply something other than the word's literal definition. This is often done by comparing two things. If you say *I felt like a butterfly when I got a new haircut*, the listener knows you don't resemble an insect but instead felt beautiful and transformed.

Word Structure

Although you are not expected to know every word in the English language for your test, you will need the ability to use deductive reasoning to find the choice that is the best match for the word in question, which is why we are going to explain how to break a word into its parts to determine its meaning. Many words can be broken down into three main parts:

prefix – root – suffix

Roots are the building blocks of all words. Every word is either a root itself or has a root. Just as a plant cannot grow without roots, neither can vocabulary, because a word must have a root to give it meaning. The root is what is left when you strip away all the prefixes and suffixes from a word. For example, in the word *unclear*, if you take away the prefix *un-*, you have the root *clear*.

Roots are not always recognizable words, because they generally come from Latin or Greek words, such as *nat*, a Latin root meaning born. The word *native*, which means a person born in a referenced placed, comes from this root, so does the word *prenatal*, meaning before birth. It's important to keep in mind, however, that roots do not always match the exact definitions of words, and they can have several different spellings.

Prefixes are syllables added to the beginning of a word and **suffixes** are syllables added to the end of the word. Both carry assigned meanings and can be attached to a word to completely change the word's meaning or to enhance the word's original meaning.

Let's use the word prefix itself as an example: *fix* means to place something securely and *pre-* means before. Therefore, *prefix* means to place something before or in front. Now let's look at a suffix: in the word *feminism*, *femin* is a root which means female. The suffix *-ism* means act, practice, or process. Thus, *feminism* is the process of establishing equal rights for women.

Although you cannot determine the meaning of a word by a prefix or suffix alone, you can use this knowledge to eliminate answer choices; understanding whether the word is positive or negative can give you the partial meaning of the word.

Reading Comprehension Practice Test

The following passage is taken from Peter Pan *by J.M. Barrie.*

I don't know whether you have ever seen a map of a person's mind. Doctors sometimes draw maps of other parts of you, and your own map can become intensely interesting, but catch them trying to draw a map of a child's mind, which is not only confused, but keeps going round all the time. There are zigzag lines on it, just like your temperature on a card, and these are probably roads in the island, for the Neverland is always more or less an island, with astonishing splashes of color here and there, and coral reefs and rakish-looking craft in the offing, and savages and lonely lairs, and gnomes who are mostly tailors, and caves through which a river runs, and princes with six elder brothers, and a hut fast going to decay, and one very small old lady with a hooked nose. It would be an easy map if that were all, but there is also first day at school, religion, fathers, the round pond, needle-work, murders, hangings, verbs that take the dative, chocolate pudding day, getting into braces, say ninety-nine, three-pence for pulling out your tooth yourself, and so on, and either these are part of the island or they are another map showing through, and it is all rather confusing, especially as nothing will stand still.

1. What is the main idea of the passage?
   A. Children's minds are simpler than adult minds.
   B. Children's minds are more complex than adult minds.
   C. No one can map the human mind.
   D. Doctors can map children's minds.

2. Which statement is not a detail from the passage?
   A. Peter Pan lives in Neverland.
   B. Neverland is more or less an island.
   C. Gnomes are mostly tailors.
   D. There is chocolate pudding day.

3. What is the meaning of <u>rakish</u> in the middle of the paragraph?
   A. Zigzag
   B. Sailing
   C. Sinking
   D. Streamlined

4. What is the author's primary purpose in writing this passage?
   A. To entertain young readers
   B. To entertain adult readers
   C. To educate children about Neverland
   D. To explain the existence of Neverland

5. Which is the best summary of this passage?
   A. Children's minds are jumbled and confusing.
   B. Adult minds are jumbled and confusing.
   C. Children think about mundane things.
   D. Children are imaginative.

This passage is taken from Sense and Sensibility *by Jane Austen.*

The situation of the house was good. High hills rose immediately behind, and at no great distance on each side; some of which were open downs, the others cultivated and woody. The village of Barton was chiefly on one of these hills, and formed a pleasant view from the cottage windows. The prospect in front was more extensive; it commanded the whole of the valley, and reached into the country beyond. The hills which surrounded the cottage terminated the valley in that direction; under another name, and in another course, it branched out again between two of the steepest of them.

With the size and furniture of the house Mrs. Dashwood was upon the whole well satisfied; for though her former style of life rendered many additions to the latter indispensable, yet to add and improve was a delight to her; and she had at this time ready money enough to supply all that was wanted of greater elegance to the apartments. "As for the house itself, to be sure," said she, "it is too small for our family, but we will make ourselves tolerably comfortable for the present, as it is too late in the year for improvements. Perhaps in the spring, if I have plenty of money, as I dare say I shall, we may think about building. These parlors are both too small for such parties of our friends as I hope to see often collected here; and I have some thoughts of throwing the passage into one of them with perhaps a part of the other, and so leave the remainder of that other for an entrance; this, with a new drawing room which may be easily added, and a bed-chamber and garret above, will make it a very snug little cottage. I could wish the stairs were handsome. But one must not expect everything; though, I suppose it would be no difficult matter to widen them. I shall see how much I am before-hand with the world in the spring, and we will plan our improvements accordingly."

6. What is the main idea of the passage?
   A. The house is well-placed.
   B. The house is too small.
   C. The house could be improved.
   D. The house is quite poor.

7. Which statement is not a detail from the passage?
   A. The parlors are too small.
   B. There is a garret above the drawing room.
   C. The cottage has hills behind it.
   D. Mrs. Dashwood has nice furnishings.

8. What is the meaning of <u>indispensable</u> in the second paragraph?
   A. Necessary
   B. Unnecessary
   C. Unappealing
   D. Appealing

9. What is the author's primary purpose in writing this passage?
   A. To create a visual impression of the house
   B. To provide insights into Mrs. Dashwood's character
   C. To show how Mrs. Dashwood felt about the cottage
   D. To illustrate Mrs. Dashwood's financial state

10. Which is the best summary of this passage?
    A. Mrs. Dashwood finds the cottage lovely, but inadequate.
    B. Mrs. Dashwood would like a smaller home.
    C. Mrs. Dashwood is quite wealthy.
    D. Mrs. Dashwood is impoverished.

This passage is taken from Myths and Legends of Ancient Greece and Rome *by E. M. Berens.*

The division of the world being now satisfactorily arranged, it would seem that all things ought to have gone on smoothly, but such was not the case. Trouble arose in an unlooked-for quarter. The Giants, those hideous monsters (some with legs formed of serpents) who had sprung from the earth and the blood of Uranus, declared war against the triumphant deities of Olympus, and a struggle ensued, which, in consequence of Gæa having made these children of hers invincible as long as they kept their feet on the ground, was wearisome and protracted. Their mother's precaution, however, was rendered unavailing by pieces of rock being hurled upon them, which threw them down, and their feet being no longer placed firmly on their mother-earth, they were overcome, and this tedious war (which was called the Gigantomachia) at last came to an end. Among the most daring of these earth-born giants were Enceladus, Rhœtus, and the valiant Mimas, who, with youthful fire and energy, hurled against heaven great masses of rock and burning oak-trees, and defied the lightning of Zeus. One of the most powerful monsters who opposed Zeus in this war was called Typhon or Typhœus. He was the youngest son of Tartarus and Gæa, and had a hundred heads, with eyes which struck terror to the beholders, and awe-inspiring voices frightful to hear. This dreadful monster resolved to conquer both gods and men, but his plans were at length defeated by Zeus, who, after a violent encounter, succeeded in destroying him with a thunderbolt, but not before he had so terrified the gods that they had fled for refuge to Egypt, where they metamorphosed themselves into different animals and thus escaped.

11. What is the main idea of the passage?
    A. Zeus had to fight the Giants
    B. Gaea was the mother of the gods.
    C. Gaea was the mother of the Giants.
    D. The Giants won the battle.

12. Which statement is not a detail from the passage?
    A. Zeus was called Typhon
    B. Zeus was the son of Gaea
    C. Zeus was the husband of Hera
    D. Zeus was the son of Tartarus

13. What is the meaning of triumphant in the paragraph?
    A. Failing
    B. Greek
    C. Victorious
    D. Immoral

14. What is the author's primary purpose in writing this passage?
    A. To entertain the reader
    B. To share stories from mythology
    C. To provide religious education
    D. To show why Greek mythology is wrong

15. Which is the best summary of this passage?

    A. The Giants were monstrous and evil.

    B. The Greek gods of Olympus had to defeat the Giants.

    C. The Giants are the precursors of the gods.

    D. Greek mythology is violent.

This passage is taken from Anne of Green Gables *by L.M. Montgomery.*

"Oh, I can carry it," the child responded cheerfully. "It isn't heavy. I've got all my worldly goods in it, but it isn't heavy. And if it isn't carried in just a certain way the handle pulls out—so I'd better keep it because I know the exact knack of it. It's an extremely old carpet-bag. Oh, I'm very glad you've come, even if it would have been nice to sleep in a wild cherry-tree. We've got to drive a long piece, haven't we? Mrs. Spencer said it was eight miles. I'm glad because I love driving. Oh, it seems so wonderful that I'm going to live with you and belong to you. I've never belonged to anybody—not really. But the asylum was the worst. I've only been in it four months, but that was enough. I don't suppose you ever were an orphan in an asylum, so you can't possibly understand what it is like. It's worse than anything you could imagine. Mrs. Spencer said it was wicked of me to talk like that, but I didn't mean to be wicked. It's so easy to be wicked without knowing it, isn't it? They were good, you know—the asylum people. But there is so little scope for the imagination in an asylum—only just in the other orphans. It was pretty interesting to imagine things about them—to imagine that perhaps the girl who sat next to you was really the daughter of a belted earl, who had been stolen away from her parents in her infancy by a cruel nurse who died before she could confess. I used to lie awake at nights and imagine things like that, because I didn't have time in the day. I guess that's why I'm so thin—I AM dreadful thin, ain't I? There isn't a pick on my bones. I do love to imagine I'm nice and plump, with dimples in my elbows.

16. What is the main idea of the passage?

    A. The girl is an orphan.

    B. The girl has been in an orphanage.

    C. The girl is excited and imaginative.

    D. The girl in the orphanage is the daughter of an earl.

17. Which statement is not a detail from the passage?

    A. The child has an old carpet-bag.

    B. The child loves driving.

    C. The child is thin.

    D. The asylum was a horrible place.

18. What is the meaning of <u>asylum</u> in the paragraph?

    A. Hospital

    B. Sanitarium

    C. Orphanage

    D. Prison

19. What is the author's primary purpose in writing this passage?

    A. To illustrate the child's excitement.

    B. To educate the reader.

    C. To explain why orphanages were bad.

    D. To create the setting.

20. Which is the best summary of this passage?

    A. The child is frightened of the changes in her life.

    B. The child is excited by the changes in her life.

    C. The family is unhappy about the child.

    D. The family is happy about the child.

Reading Comprehension Practice Test Answer Key

1. B
2. A
3. D
4. A
5. A
6. C
7. B
8. A
9. C
10. A
11. A
12. C
13. C
14. B
15. B
16. C
17. D
18. C
19. A
20. B

Chapter Six: Mathematics Skills Test

The Math Skills Test section tests various concepts in numbers and operations, algebra, geometry, data analysis, statistics, and probability. In this test section, you will be provided 40 minutes to answer a varying number of questions. This is an adaptive test section, so the number of questions you answer depends on whether you answered previous questions correctly or not. Do NOT guess on questions unless you absolutely are stuck, and even then do your best to eliminate wrong choices first. Before taking the SIFT, you want to make sure that you have a good understanding of the math areas covered. You will need to sharpen your skills, but don't worry – we'll provide you with the knowledge that you'll need to know for the test. We have 50 practice questions, which will give you an opportunity to hone your skills on the different concepts. Remember to take your time, accuracy is paramount on the Math Skills Test since you cannot go back and change answers!

Numbers

Whole Numbers

Most people know what whole numbers are, even if you do not know the term "whole number". A whole number is exactly what it sounds like: an *entire* number. Examples of whole numbers are 0, 1, 2, 3, 4, and so on. There is no decimal or fractional part. Whole numbers are part of a system that is known as the place value system. In this system, numbers are labeled with specific words, depending on their position.

You may have heard the term "counting numbers" or "natural numbers," which are whole numbers without the "0". Natural numbers are often used for basic counting, ordering, and things of that nature. These numbers are the simplest form of numbers, from which other number sets are created.

Here is a brief table you can use to refresh your memory and better grasp this concept:

Value	Place
One	1
Ten	10
Hundred	100
Thousand	1,000
Ten thousand	10,000
Hundred thousand	100,000
Million	1,000,000

This decimal number system (also called base 10 since it has 10 as its base) continues into the millions and beyond.

If you were given a number such as 14,567, the word associated with it would be fourteen thousand, five hundred and sixty-seven. It is important to grasp this concept because on the arithmetic reasoning portion of the ASVAB, you may encounter numbers as their long-form versions rather than the punctual versions you are used to.

Rounding is a term that is used to quickly determine the relative size of a whole number based on a new number (either larger or smaller than the original number). Rounding is the best method to approximate numbers quickly.

Here is the general procedure for rounding:

❖ Choose the digit you will be rounding and underline it (so you know which one it is).

❖ Look at the digit directly to the right of the digit you are rounding. If that number is less than 5, then you will leave the underlined digit alone. If the digit to the right of the digit you are rounding is 5 or more, then you will add 1 to the digit you are rounding.

❖ Last, replace all of the digits that are to the right of the underlined digit with 0's (up to the decimal point).

EXAMPLE

Round 356,782 to the nearest ten thousand.

First, you will select the ten-thousands spot, the 5. Then you will look at the number to the right of it, the 6. That number is larger than 4, so you add one to the 5 spot, giving you 366,472. Now you will replace numbers to the right of the primary digit with 0's, giving you 360,000.

Prime Numbers

Prime numbers are numbers that have only two factors, 1 and itself. Examples would include 2, 3, 5, 7, 11, 13, 17, 19, and 23, as well as many others. When you are attempting to figure out if a number is a prime number or not, all you need to do is figure out whether other numbers, besides 1 and the number itself, will divide evenly into it.

EXAMPLES

1. Is 66 a prime number?

66 is not a prime number. It can be divided by 2 and 33, 3 and 22, 6 and 11, as well as 1 and 66.

2. Is 21 a prime number?

21 is not a prime number, since 7 and 3 will divide into it, as well as 1 and 21.

It is important to note that prime numbers are typically odd, with the exception of the number 2. Even numbers clearly can be divided by 2, so even numbers larger than 2 will never be prime.

Mean (Average), Standard Deviation, Median, and Mode

You may be asked to find the **mean, standard deviation, median,** or **mode** of a set of numbers. The mean (average) of numbers is obtained by adding up all the numbers and then dividing by the number of numbers that you added up. The standard deviation is a measurement (which you probably won't have to compute!) of how far apart the numbers are from the mean or average. The median is obtained by ordering the numbers and picking the middle number, or averaging the two middle numbers. The mode is obtained by finding the number repeated the most number of times (if there is a number that repeats).

Multiples

Multiples of numbers are what results from multiplying whole numbers by other numbers. For example, multiples of 7 are 7, 14, 21, and so on.

Common multiples of two numbers are the numbers that are multiples of both. If you were looking at, for example, 4 and 8, then 16 would be a common multiple. 8 would also be a common multiple of the two numbers.

The least common multiple is the smallest common multiple that two given numbers share. The fastest way to find this is to just write out the first few multiples for both numbers that you have available and then figure out which one is the smallest. This is not a particularly difficult task, but you will have to understand how multiples work in order to do it properly. For example, the least common multiple of 4 and 8 is 8.

Factors

A **factor** is a number that goes evenly into another number with no remainder. So think of factors as all the numbers you can multiply together to get another number. Here is an example:

What are the factors of 24?

1 and 24, 2 and 12, 3 and 8, 4 and 6, since all of these numbers go into 24 exactly (without a remainder).

It is not necessary to write them like that, but it will help you keep them in mind if you keep the factors together with their counterparts. Another way to write these is 1, 2, 3, 4, 6, 8, 12, and 24.

If you want to figure out whether a number is a factor of another one or not, just divide the number by the potential factor and see if the result is a whole number. Every number will have at least two factors, 1 and the number itself. For example, the two factors of 2 are 1 and 2.

Common Factors

Numbers that are the factors of more than one whole number are known as **common factors**. For example, 6 would be a common factor of both 12 and 24 (because it can be multiplied by 2 to reach 12 and 4 to reach 24). The largest factor that goes into two numbers is called the greatest common factor.

Exponents

Exponents and exponential notation are used to help simply expressions, particularly when factors are repeated multiple times. Exponents are written as superscripts above the number that has the exponent. The number that has the exponent is called the base, so 8 is the base and 2 is the exponent in this example:

$$8 \times 8 = 8^2$$

Think of exponents as shorthand that is used to help keep the math straight and stop it from becoming too confusing. This can be seen below:

$$5 \times 5 \times 5 \times 5 \times 5 \times 5 = 5^6$$

Writing the number as an exponent makes it much easier to see what is happening and will simplify equations for you. Another way to say what is happening above is "five to the sixth power" or "five to the sixth". Here is another example where we are simplifying with an exponent:

$$2 + 2 \times 5 \times 5 \times 6 \times 7 + 8 = 2 + 2 \times 5^2 \times 6 \times 7 + 8$$

Does it simplify that equation a lot? Not in this case, but it does make it a little bit simpler to read.

Exponents are also used to denote cumbersome numbers in scientific notation; for example, $54000 = 5.4 \times 10^4$ and $.0043 = 4.3 \times 10^{-3}$.

Let's say a few words about fractional exponents and negative exponents. In an exponent that is a fraction, the number on the top acts just like an exponent, but the number on the bottom designates a "root" (see next section), which means a number would have to multiplied that many times to get to that number. For example, $8^{2/3} = (\sqrt[3]{8^2}) = (\sqrt[3]{8})^2 = 2 \times 2 = 4$. With negative exponents, you have to take the reciprocal of the base and make the exponent positive. For example, $2^{-3} = (\frac{1}{2})^3 = \frac{1}{8}$.

Also note that you can use exponents for questions dealing with combinations of letters or numbers. For example, if you were asked how many different numbers on a license plate there could be if the first three digits were letters, and the last 4 were numbers $0 - 9$, you'd have $26^3 \times 10^4$, since there are 3 places for 26 letters and 4 places for 10 numbers.

Square Roots

The term "**square root**" is used to describe a number that can be squared to equal the number provided.

The radical sign ($\sqrt{}$) is used to show square roots. For example, $\sqrt{9} = 3$, since $3^2 = 9$.

Some numbers will have very clean whole numbers for their roots. These are known as perfect squares. Here is a table that shows common perfect squares:

Number	Perfect Square	Square Root
1	1	$\sqrt{1}$
2	4	$\sqrt{4}$
3	9	$\sqrt{9}$
4	16	$\sqrt{16}$
5	25	$\sqrt{25}$
6	36	$\sqrt{36}$
7	49	$\sqrt{49}$
8	64	$\sqrt{64}$
9	81	$\sqrt{81}$
10	100	$\sqrt{100}$

Note that if we wanted the number that is multiplied 3 times to get a certain number, this is the cube root, so $\sqrt[3]{8} = 2$. We can use this same notation for 4th roots, and so on.

Fractions and Decimals

Fractions and decimals are both methods of elaborating on *parts* of whole numbers. This is usually illustrated by two numbers, say 0 and 1, and then viewing them via a line between them. That line represents all of the fractions or decimals in between those two numbers.

Take **fractions** first. The most basic way to view a fraction is to look at it as parts of a whole. The division sign ("/" or "−"), which separate the two numbers, can represent the words "out of". So if you have $\frac{2}{4}$, you have 2 out of 4 parts, which is actually the same as 1 out of 2 parts. For example:

In the above image, you can see that there are 4 parts (rectangular boxes). Of these, 2 of them are black. So you have $\frac{2}{4}$ boxes that are black. Note that this also represents $\frac{1}{2}$ of the boxes, and we can say that $\frac{2}{4}$ reduces or simplifies to $\frac{1}{2}$.

The top part of the fraction is called the "numerator" and the bottom part is called the "denominator". When looking at fractions, if the numerator is less than the denominator, it is referred to as a *proper fraction*. The value of these types of fractions is less than 1. Some examples of proper fractions are $\frac{3}{9}$ or $\frac{1}{3}$, $\frac{2}{5}$, and $\frac{8}{19}$.

If the numerator is equal to or greater than the denominator, then you have an *improper fraction*. Some examples of improper fractions are $\frac{6}{3}$ or $\frac{2}{1}$ (which is 2), $\frac{8}{3}$ and $\frac{5}{2}$. . Any improper fraction can be written in the form of a mixed number, and any mixed number can be written in the form of an improper fraction. For example, $\frac{4}{3}$ is the same as $\frac{3}{3} + \frac{1}{3} = 1\frac{1}{3}$.

It should be noted that with fractions, $\frac{4}{4}$ is the same as 1, $\frac{8}{4}$ is the same as 2, and $\frac{9}{3}$ is the same as 3; these pairs of fractions are "equivalent". (See how if we were to multiply both the numerator and denominator by the same number, we will get equivalent fractions?). Likewise, $\frac{6}{4}$ is the same as $\frac{3}{2}$ which equals $1\frac{1}{2}$. This is how fractions are converted back and forth into whole numbers and mixed fractions.

To review:

❖ **Proper fractions** – These are fractions with a value of less than 1. The numerator is smaller than the denominator. $\frac{1}{2}$ is an example.

❖ **Improper fractions** – These are fractions with a value of 1 or more. The numerator is larger than the denominator. $\frac{7}{5}$ is an example.

❖ **Mixed numbers** – These are whole numbers that are combined with fractions. $5\frac{1}{2}$ is an example.

Now onto **decimals**. Everything talked about earlier, in terms of whole numbers, have included digits that are powers of 10, but greater than 1 (to the left-hand side of the decimal point). Again, the number system is a "base 10" system. Decimals are a kind of shorthand that are used to help describe base 10 numbers (fractions of a whole number) that are on the right-hand side of the decimal point, which means they are less than 1.

Here is a table that might help explain this concept a bit better. Notice that the names of the places to the right of the decimal include a "th" at the end:

Place	Decimal
Tenth	0.1
Hundredth	0.01
Thousandth	0.001

In this way, you can describe numbers smaller than whole numbers in a method other than using fractions. This is also how percents are written (see the next section). So if you have 0.5, you have exactly $\frac{1}{2}$ of 1. You can also think of this as $\frac{5}{10}$, or $\frac{1}{2}$, or $\frac{.5}{1}$, which is five-tenths of 1.

Note: Remember that typically in fractions and percent problems, "of" represents multiplication; for example, $\frac{1}{2}$ of 4 = $\frac{1}{2} \times 4 = 2$.

Percents can be considered fractions that have a bottom number (denominator) equal to 100. You can think of this as "per hundred", which is what "percent" actually means. The symbol that is used to denote a percent is %. For example:

$\frac{50}{100}$ is the same thing as .50 is the same thing as 50%.

You can see that there is a very clear and definite relationship among fractions, decimals, and percents. Percents are typically used in order to describe portions of a whole, just like the other two are. If you have a fraction, you can convert the top and bottom numbers to $\frac{\#}{100}$ in order to determine the percent. Likewise, you can simply shift the decimal two places to the right to get a percent from a decimal; for example, 0.75 is 75%. To get a decimal from a percent, shift the decimal two places to the left; for example, 45% is .45.

A typical question about percents on the ASVAB might be converting them to decimals and back to percents.

Operations

Operations are the calculations that are done to numbers. The *Fundamental Operations of Arithmetic*, as they are called, are addition, subtraction, multiplication, and division. Solving the problems in the ASVAB will require you to perform these operations on whole numbers, decimals, and fractions.

Addition and Subtraction

The **addition** of whole numbers is not too complicated. Adding two numbers together is an operation that results in a total that is known as the sum. The very first step here is to line up the numbers you are going to add by their place value. All of the ones will go in a line (column), and then tens, hundreds, thousands, and so on. Once this has been done, you will add the columns together. Any time the sum of a column reaches 10, you need to carry over the 10 as a single digit to the next column to the left. So 10 in the ones column would be 1 in the tens column. Proceed to do this until the numbers have been added up.

EXAMPLE

Add together 20, 15, 2, and 107.

```
  +1
   20
   15
    2
+ 107
  144
```

Now look at those numbers. The digits in the ones column (the right-most column) add up to 14. Bring down the 4 to the ones digit and carry over the 10 to the next column (to the left). So 2 + 1 + 1 (the carryover) + 0 = 4. So there is a 4 in the tens digit as well. The hundreds column only has a 1. So the final result is 144.

Adding together decimals is the exact same procedure. The only change is that you have to deal with that pesky decimal point. All you have to do is line up the decimal point vertically with every single number you need to add. You then add them together just like before to get your sum. For whole numbers, you can make this easier by adding a decimal point to the right of the number (so 17 would become 17.0 or 17.00, for example, depending on how long the other decimals are).

If you want to make things easier, you can just put 0s in the place of any empty spots to make it easier to add together.

EXAMPLE

Add together 13.2, 0.54, 2, and 0.008.

```
  13.2
  0.54
  2
+ 0.008
```

The best way to do this is to modify the numbers a little bit. Note that they are still the same numbers, but easier to add:

```
  13.200
  00.540
  02.000
+ 00.008
  15.748
```

You can readily see that this small procedure makes these numbers much easier to add together. Adding them will give you 15.748.

Subtraction is the inverse or opposite of addition. It could also be considered another form of addition (by adding negative numbers), but that concept will be covered in a later section. Subtracting a number from another number will give you a result that is known as the difference. The steps are the same but backward. Line up the two numbers like before. (You should only subtract two numbers at a time). If the number on top is less than the one on the bottom for that column, then "borrow" from the next column (the one to the left) and continue with the operation.

EXAMPLES

1. Subtract 108 from 110.

```
  110
- 108
    2
```

Start with the right-most column, the ones column. Since 8 is greater than 0, you have to borrow from the tens column to turn the 0 into a 10 before you subtract. But then you have to turn the 1 in the tens column into a 0 (subtract 1 in the tens column). So the final answer is just 2. Again, like addition, this is a pretty simple process that most individuals are already used to doing without even thinking about it.

The subtraction of decimals, again, is much the same as the addition of decimals. Before subtracting, you have to line up the decimal points of the numbers that are being subtracted from one another and then place the decimal point below those two amounts in the same spot.

2. Subtract 89.3 from 109.4.

109.45
– 89.3

The first thing you want to do is fill in any zeroes to the right of the decimal point. In this case, we don't need to borrow.

109.45
– 089.30
20.10

Practice makes perfect when it comes to addition and subtraction. Spend a little bit of time working on these types of problems on your own. The more you do it, the easier it will become. It would benefit you greatly to do these types of problems on paper without the use of a calculator. This will help you with mental calculations and will greatly increase your accuracy. There are a lot of websites that provide practice on these types of problems.

Multiplication

Multiplication is the next basic operation that you will need to know for the ASVAB. The multiplication of two numbers, which is basically repeated addition, will result in a number that is known as the product. The very first step in multiplication is putting the number with the most digits on top and lining up the numbers to the right. There are two general situations you will encounter when you have to multiply two numbers together.

1. One of the numbers you have to multiple has only a single digit. For example multiplying 15 by 8.
2. Both of the numbers you have to multiply have more than one digit. For example multiplying 10 by 16.

In the first situation, you want to put the number with the single digit on the bottom and then multiply all of the digits of the top number by the bottom number. You will begin on the right-hand side of the top number and then multiply individual digits, working to the left. If the multiplication results in a number with more than one digit, you will write down the ones digit in the product and carry the tens digit to the next column. Then you will add the carried number to the next multiplication.

EXAMPLES

1. Multiple 123 by 6.

```
  123
×   6
```

Notice how the number with the most digit is put on top. The first step would be to look at the singles digit (6). Multiple that number (6) by the rightmost number in the top column (3). That will result in 18, so we'll put an 8 below. Moving left, the 6 is multiplied by 2 (on a diagonal), resulting in 12, but we also have to add the 1 that we just carried, so we get 13. Put a 3 below, and carry 1. Now the 6 is multiplied by the 1 to get 6, but we need to carry over the 1 from the 13, so we get 7. The final result is 738.

```
   123
×   6
   738
```

The second situation is the same as the first, but with an additional step. Again, remember to place the number with the most digits on top, and start multiplying from the right (the ones digits). You will first multiple the ones column by the top number, then the tens, then the hundreds, and so on until you are finished. Each value place you move to the left will add a zero to the right of the product. The products will then be added together to give the final result.

2. Multiply 201 by 13.

```
    201
×    13
    603
+  2010
   2613
```

The first thing that has so be done after arranging the numbers in the correct way is to multiply 3 by 1 to get 3. Then multiply 3 by 0 and 3 by 2, respectively, for a result of 603 total. Now you will do the same thing with the 1 (the tens digit of the second number). 1 times 201 is, obviously, 201. But since you are using the tens digit, add a 0 to the right-hand side of this number, giving you 2010. This is to reflect the higher value of the digit being multiplied. Now, finally, you will add the 603 and 2010, giving you a final result of 2613.

The multiplication of decimals requires something quite different than what you did during the addition and subtraction. In this situation, you will completely *ignore* the decimal point altogether. Multiply the two numbers together as if they were whole numbers. Once you are done doing that, you will figure out where to place the decimal point back in. This sounds much more difficult than it actually is.

3. Multiply 54.8 by 9.9.

```
   54.8
×  9.9
```

First, you will take out the decimal points so that the multiplication will be a bit simpler.

$$548$$
$$\times\ 99$$

Now finish up the multiplication and addition as we did earlier:

```
      +4 +7
       548
  ×     99
      4932
 +   49320
     54252
```

To deal with the decimal points, add up the number of digits to the right of the decimal points in the original numbers. This does *not* mean to add up the actual numbers; it means add the number of total digits to the right of the decimal points. So 54.8 has one digit to the right of the decimal point and 9.9 has one digit to the right of the decimal point. This means you have 1 + 1 digits to the right of the decimal points (2). In the final product, 54252, just stick the decimal point in (from the right) based on that number. The result would be 542.52.

This process is a bit more complicated than the simple addition and subtraction that was done earlier and it is also more complicated than the multiplication of whole numbers. Regardless, it will get a lot easier once you have done it a few times.

Division

Division is the process of splitting a number into parts or groups, and this yields a quotient. There are four basic steps that you will undertake to do long division and you will repeat these steps for every division operation that you have to perform.

EXAMPLE

Divide 5 into 65.

The first step here is going to be to set up the problem:

65/5 or $5\sqrt{65}$

Now you will begin the actual division. First, select the leftmost digit of the number being divided (the dividend) and see how many times the divisor goes into it. In this case, 5 goes into 6 one (1) time. 6 – 5 is 1, leaving a remainder of 1. Now you will take the remainder, along with the next digit in the number being divided, in this case 1 and 5 respectively, and see how many times the divisor goes into it. How many times does 5 go into 15? The answer is 3. Pair that with the original digit you got and you have your solution: 13.

```
        1 3
  5√6 5
      5 0
      1 5
      1 5
        0
```

To test your answer, multiply 13 by 5 and see what you get. Is it the original number, 65? Yes, it is. So the division is correct. Always test once this has been done, and remember to add any remainder you might get to the product of the divisor and dividend when checking your answer.

When doing this with decimals, you will work exactly as you did with multiplication. Ignore the decimals until the end and then deal with them just like before. Add the decimal in exactly where it would be in the number that is being divided (move the decimal straight up into the answer). However, if there is a decimal in the outside (divisor), you must move the decimal to the right to make this a whole number, and then do the same (same number of places) on the inside (the dividend). Then you move the decimal straight up.

Order of Operations

The **order of operations** is the way that multiple operations need to be done in order to reach the correct answer. Some operations take precedence over others; mathematical operations don't also go from left to right, like reading does.

Here is the basic order of operations:
1. First take care of any operations that are within a grouping symbol such as parentheses () or brackets [].
2. Next handle the roots and the exponents.
3. Next handle the multiplication and division in the same order that they appear (left to right).
4. Finally, handle the addition and subtraction (again, moving from left to right).

As an example, consider the following:

$$\text{Solve: } 2 + 2 \times 2$$

If you ignore the order of operations, what do you get?

$$2 + 2 \times 2 = 4 \times 2 = 8$$

Now if you were to follow the order of operations, what happens?

$$2 + 2 \times 2 = 2 + 4 = 6$$

We get two different answers, but only the second is correct, since we need to perform multiplication before addition. It is important to eliminate any ambiguous statements in equations, because precision is key. That is why the order of operations is very important.

There is an acronym that can be used to help you remember the order of operations using PEMDAS: Parentheses, Exponents, Multiplication/Division, Addition/Subtraction.

If you are using PEMDAS, you need to remember that multiplication and division have to be completed as one step from left to right, and the same with addition and subtraction.

Working with Integers

Integers is a set that includes all whole numbers and the negatives (opposites) of those numbers as well. For example, integers are:

$$... - 3, - 2, - 1, 0, 1, 2, 3 ...$$

Think of adding negative numbers as the same as subtracting positive numbers. For example,

$$6 + {-5} = 6 - 5 = 1$$

Addition and Subtraction with Positives and Negatives

There are two situations you will encounter when you have to add integers with negative sign(s). Are the numbers the same sign or are the numbers opposite signs? If the numbers are the same, then you can just add them like you normally would, and then add a negative sign to the answer if the two signs were negative to start out with. Here are a few example situations:

$$3 + 3 = 6$$

$$-3 + {-3} = -6$$

So how do you handle a situation when the two numbers have different signs? Ignore the signs, subtract the smaller from the larger, and then use the sign of the greater of the two numbers. Here are a few examples:

$3 + {-4} = -1$: 4 is greater than 3, so use the sign before the 4 (negative) in the answer

$-5 + 4 = 1$: 5 is greater than 4, so use sign before the 5 (positive) in the answer

If you are subtracting, and have two negatives together, change them into one positive:

$$2 - {-2} = 2 + 2 = 4$$

In all, the best way to handle subtraction with negative numbers is to just turn the problem into an addition problem.

You may also need to know that the **absolute value** (signified by $|\ \ |$) is the positive equivalent of positive and negative numbers. So $|-4| = 4$ and $|4| = 4$. So a number and the absolute value of its negative counterpart are equal.

Multiplication and Division with Positives and Negatives

Again, the best way to handle this is to ignore the signs and then multiply or divide like you normally would. To figure out what sign the final product will have, you simply have to figure out how many negatives are in the numbers you worked with. If the number of negatives is even, the result will be a positive number. If the number of negatives is odd, the result will be a negative number. For example:

$2 \times 2 \times {-2} = -8$:   one negative: odd number of negatives, so negative

$-2 \times -2 \times 2 = 8:$ two negatives: even number of negatives, so positive

$-2 \times -2 \times -2 = -8:$ three negatives: odd number of negatives, so negative

Exponents of Negative Numbers

Exponents with negative numbers are relatively simple: If the number with the exponent (the base) is negative and the exponent is even, the result will be positive. If the number with the exponent is negative and the exponent is odd, the result will be negative. This is because, for example, $-4 \times -4 \times -4 \times -4 = 256$, but $-4 \times -4 \times -4 = -64$.

But we have to be careful with negative bases and even exponents. For even exponents, if the base is negative and in parentheses (or is a variable that you're putting in a number in for), the result is positive. For even exponents, if the negative sign is outside the parentheses, you have to raise the base to the exponent first, and then apply the negative (change the sign). Here are some examples:

$$(-4)^2 = 16$$
$$-4^2 = -(4^2) = -16$$
$$(-3)^3 = -27$$
$$-3^3 = -(3^2) = -27$$

Evaluate x^2, where $x = -2$: $(-2)^2 = 4$

Evaluate $-x^4$, where $x = -2$: $-(-2)^4 = -16$

And again, remember that exponents are just another way of writing out multiplication.

Working with Fractions

Check the arithmetic review section of this guide for information on how to convert fractions back and forth. This section will cover different types of fractions and how to perform operations on fractions.

Equivalent Fractions

Equivalent fractions are fractions that are equal. One of the most common things that you will do when you are working with fractions is to simplify them. Another way to state this is to "reduce" fractions. All this means is writing the fraction in the smallest equivalent fraction you can (smallest top and bottom). For example, $\frac{5}{10}$ and $\frac{2}{4}$ can both be simplified to $\frac{1}{2}$. So $\frac{5}{10}, \frac{2}{4},$ and $\frac{1}{2}$ are all equivalent fractions.

Here are some things to keep in mind when you are trying to simplify fractions:
 ❖ You need to find a number that can evenly divide into the top and the bottom number of the fraction that you are simplifying. After that, you can do the actual division.

- Once the division is finished, check to make sure your fraction cannot be further simplified. It is easy to make this mistake; even if you have found an equivalent fraction, it may be completely simplified, and your answer could be wrong.
- You can use simplification to reduce fractions to lower terms by dividing the top and bottom by the same number. You can also, perhaps more importantly, raise fractions to higher terms if you multiply both the top and the bottom numbers by the same number. This is very important in the addition and subtraction of fractions.

Here is an example of reducing a fraction:

$$\frac{6}{9} = \frac{2}{3}$$

The largest number you can divide into both of the numbers in the fraction (6 and 9) is 3. $\frac{6}{3} = 2$ and $\frac{9}{3} = 3$, giving the new fraction: $\frac{2}{3}$.

Here is an example of raising a fraction:

$$\frac{2}{4} = \frac{4}{8}$$

Simply multiply the 2 and the 4 each by 2 and you get the new equivalent fraction: $\frac{4}{8}$.

Addition and Subtraction

To add and subtract fractions, you need to understand two terms:
- **Numerator** – The number on the top of a fraction.
- **Denominator** – The number on the bottom of a fraction.

If you have two numbers that have the same denominator, you will have what is known as a common denominator. You can really only add or subtract fractions that have a common denominator, so if you do not have one, you need to make one, using equivalent fractions.

Here are the steps for adding and subtracting fractions:
1. If the fractions have a common denominator, then proceed as usual. If not, then reduce or raise one or both fractions until you have a common denominator.
2. Add or subtract the numerators as you would any number, ignoring the denominator.
3. Place the resulting sum (or difference) on top of the common denominator as the new numerator.
4. Simplify the new fraction as much as possible.

Step 1 is involved with coming up with what is known as the least common denominator. This is the smallest number that all fractions have as a common denominator. The process of doing this is the same as the process for finding the least common multiple.

You can turn mixed numbers into improper fractions before adding, for example:

$$2\frac{1}{2} + 3\frac{3}{4} = \frac{5}{2} + \frac{15}{4} = \frac{10}{4} + \frac{15}{4} = \frac{25}{4} = 6\frac{1}{4}$$

You can also add the whole number parts, then add the fractional parts, and then add the two together. This will save you a lot of trouble and extra steps. It is just as correct as any other method of solving the problem and, of course, remember that you are not being tested on how you did it, just that it was done. Here is the same problem:

$$2\frac{1}{2} + 3\frac{3}{4} = 2 + \frac{1}{2} + 3 + \frac{3}{4} = 2 + 3 + \frac{1}{2} + \frac{3}{4} = 2 + 3 + \frac{2}{4} + \frac{3}{4} = 5\frac{5}{4} = 6\frac{1}{4}$$

You do have to be careful subtracting mixed numbers, since you may have to borrow:

$$2\frac{1}{4} - 1\frac{1}{2} = 2\frac{1}{4} - 1\frac{2}{4} = 1\frac{5}{4} - 1\frac{2}{4} = \frac{3}{4}$$

A simpler way may be to turn mixed fractions into improper fractions:

$$2\frac{1}{4} - 1\frac{1}{2} = \frac{9}{4} - \frac{3}{2} = \frac{9}{4} - \frac{6}{4} = \frac{3}{4}$$

Multiplication and Division

Multiplication and division of fractions is actually simpler than adding or subtracting them. When you have to multiply fractions together, you'll first want to turn any mixed fractions into improper fractions. Then you just multiply the numerators to get the new numerator and then multiply the denominators to get the new denominator. Once that is done, you can go ahead and simplify.

For example:

$$2\frac{1}{5} \times \frac{3}{7} = \frac{11}{5} \times \frac{3}{7} = \frac{11 \times 3}{5 \times 7} = \frac{33}{35}$$

There is no way to simplify $\frac{33}{35}$, so this is the final answer.

Division is a little bit more complicated, but ultimately it is the same procedure. First, you have to find the reciprocal of the second fraction. A reciprocal is a fraction that is "flipped": its numerator and denominator are switched. Once that is done, you will multiply the fractions as usual.

Here is an example:

$$\frac{5}{6} \div \frac{2}{3} = \frac{5}{6} \times \frac{3}{2} = \frac{5 \times 3}{6 \times 2} = \frac{15}{12} = \frac{5}{4}$$

As you can see, the second fraction $(\frac{2}{3})$ simply flips to $\frac{3}{2}$. The common way this is explained is to "flip and multiply". That is as good an explanation as any, and is certainly easier to remember. Again, you are being tested on your ability to do the math here, not to know the jargon.

Word Problems

Basic Problems

The most basic problems that you will encounter on the arithmetic reasoning section of the SIFT are problems that require one or two steps to complete. Generally, the most difficult part about these types of problems is figuring out what they are actually asking you to do.

One or two step problems usually have only one computation that needs to be made. At times, you may have to do problems that are a bit more complex. With that being said, the question you are being asked will usually be clear and not hard to figure out. The way these problems will be discussed and taught here will involve logic and examples. The exact computations will be up to you to complete on your own. And take advantage of the fact that the answers are provided by plugging them in backwards, if you need to.

EXAMPLES

1. Sally is going to the store and she is buying her groceries for the week. She is buying some apples for $5.00, some pears for $4.25, and some grapes for $9.50. How much does she spend at the store during this trip?

This is a very simple problem. It is one basic step and only involves basic arithmetic. Three numbers are provided: $5.00, $4.25, and $9.50. The question asks you how much she spends. The way to solve this is to sum the three numbers, giving you a total of $18.75. Simple, right?

2. John has a job laying tile with his father's company. He is paid $9 an hour. He works for two weeks per pay period. This period, he works 10 hours during the first week and 5 hours during the second week. How much did John make during this pay period?

This problem is a bit more complex since two operations are used. The information you are given lays it all out: He gets $9 an hour, a pay period is 2 weeks, he worked 10 hours the first week and 5 hours the second week. That's 15 total hours. 15 hours times $9 per hour yields $135 for this two-week pay period. You can also solve this by multiplying 10 hours by $9 and then 5 hours by $9 and adding them together. The result will be the same, even though the process is different.

Percent and Interest

The most common types of problems that you will encounter in the real world (in terms of word problems for mathematics) are going to be dealing with money. This is when **percent and interest** operations come into play. Either you will be dealing with interest that is being accrued on some amount of money in the bank or on a loan you are paying, or you will be trying to find a certain percentage of a sum. These two things are typically related.

Here are two things to keep in mind when you begin working on this type of problem:

❖ The first thing you need to do is to convert the percentage into a whole number or decimal. You can do this by removing the percentage and moving the decimal two places to the left. (Remember, when you are removing the percent, move the decimal away from it.)

❖ The second thing you need to do is multiply the decimal (originally the percentage) by the figure being calculated.

❖ Finally, if necessary, add the percentage amount (which is now a whole number or decimal) to the original amount.

EXAMPLE

You have an investment account and you have put in $6,000. The account earns 7.5% interest annually. How much money do you have, in total, when one year is up?

The first thing you want to do is determine the important numbers here. Beginning amount = 6000, interest for one year = 7.5% (or 0.075).

You can do this in one of two ways. You can set it up like a standard multiplication problem and then do the addition, or you can set it up in one step. Here is the first way:

$$\$6000 \times 0.075 = 450$$

$$\$6000 + \$450 = \$6450$$

In this method, you do the multiplication to get the interest added for one year, and then add this to the original sum.

The second method saves a step by combining the interest and the original amount:

$$\$6000 \times 1.075 = \$6450$$

Again, when you are dealing with percentages, it is important to convert them in the proper way by moving the decimal two places to the left when removing the percentage; for example, 10% is 0.10 and 5% is 0.05. Percentages between 1% and 99% take up the first two digits to the right of the decimal point in a conversion.

Ratios and Proportions

Ratios involve comparisons between numbers, and **proportions** involve the equalities of ratios. Ratios are usually written with a ":" separating them. So a 5 to 1 ratio would be written 5:1. These can be written fractionally as well, which is useful when you begin working with some of the word problems that involve actual proportions. For example, 5:1 would be $\frac{5}{1}$. Comparing two numbers using a ratio results (with a 1 on the bottom typically) is what is known as a unit rate. This is where you get terms like "miles per hour" or "kilometers per hour" since "per" can mean "divided by". (This is the same as finishing the division of a fractional form of a ratio).

EXAMPLE

You want to figure out how much you are paying for your flour. On the price tag, it says that the flour is $9.95 and that the bag contains 6 ounces of flour. How much does the flour cost on a per ounce basis?

You want the cost of one ounce of flour, but you are given the cost of six ounces. Turn this rate into a fraction, and then set up a proportion with ounces on the left and money on the right: $\frac{1}{6} = \frac{x}{9.95}$. You can cross-multiply to get $6x = 9.95$, so the final result is: total = $1.66 (rounded to the nearest cent).

All problems of this type will be solved in roughly the same way, as you will see when you begin doing them for yourself.

Problems of Measurement

Measurement problems are extremely simple. Typically, you are going to be asked to determine either the area or the perimeter of a given shape.

- ❖ **Perimeter** – The perimeter is the distance around the geometric shape.
- ❖ **Area** – The area is the total amount of space inside of the geometric shape.

The formula for finding **perimeter** is both of the lengths added with both of the widths: $P = l + l + w + w$, or $P = 2l + 2w$, where:

- ❖ l = length
- ❖ w = width
- ❖ P = perimeter

The formula for **area** is length times width: $A = l * w$, where:

- ❖ l = length
- ❖ w = width
- ❖ A = area

Algebra

Algebra is a method of generalizing expressions involved in arithmetic. You will be able to explain how groups of things are handled all the time. This is useful for times when you have a certain function that you need to do over and over again. In algebra, you typically have numbers as well as symbols (usually letters) called "variables" that can be used to stand for certain numbers. Typically, variables are useful when dealing with word problems, since algebra makes it easier to solve for an "unknown."

Evaluating Numbers

Numbers that are assigned a definite value (like the number "1") are constants. When symbols (variables) are used to stand for numbers, they can typically take on any number. If you saw the equation: $2x = 6$, x would be the variable here, and in this case it would equal 3.

A few things to keep in mind:

- ❖ You can make a variable anything you want. X, y, Z, a, A, b, and so on are examples. They are usually italicized, to distinguish them from numbers.
- ❖ Both sides of the = sign are, obviously, =. So you can add or subtract or multiply or divide anything on both sides (constants or variables or both), as long as you do it to both sides. This is how you solve equations. With inequalities, however, you must change the sign if you multiply or divide by a negative number.
- ❖ Many times, you must distribute either variables or constants through to get rid of parentheses. For example, if you have $3(x - 9)$, you'll want "push through" the 3 to make it $3x - 27$.

❖ Once you have figured out what a variable is, plug it into the original equation to make sure everything is still equal.

❖ You may be asked to evaluate a function for a certain value in the variable. Just plug in that value everywhere the variable is. For example, the value of $f(3)$ in the function $f(x) = 3x + 2$ is $3(3) + 2 = 11$.

Equations

Equations are expressions that have an equal sign, such as $2 + 2 = 4$. Equations will usually have a variable, and will always be true or false. $2 + 2 = 1$ is false. $2 + 2 = 4$ is true. When you are solving for variables, there will typically only be one answer that will make the equation true. That is the number you must find.

Basically, to do this, you will just rewrite the equation in more and more simple terms until you have the solution to it. Ideally, you want this to be x (or whatever variable) = a number.

$$x = \#$$

Again, you can do anything to an equation as long as you do the same thing to both sides. This is how you solve equations.

Here is an example showing this:

$$3(x - 2) = -7 + 10$$

First, simplify anything you can on one side (the −7 and 10) and also get rid of any parentheses by "pushing through" (the "3" on the left hand side):

$$3x - 6 = 3$$

Next, add 6 to both sides to get the "$3x$" by itself:

$$3x - 6 + 6 = 3 + 6$$

$$3x = 9$$

Now, simplify this by dividing both sides of the equation by 3. Note: You have to divide the *entire* side by 3, not just one part of it:

$$\frac{3x}{3} = \frac{9}{3}$$

$$x = 3$$

Now, we have x all by itself on one side; the equation is now solved.

Note that if we have an **inequality** instead of an equation, we have to be careful. We solve an inequality the same way, but if we multiply or divide by a negative number, we have to switch the sign.

For example:

$$-3x - 2 \geq 4$$

$$-3x - 2 + 2 \geq 4 + 2$$

$$-3x \geq 6$$

$$\frac{-3x}{-3} \leq \frac{6}{-3}$$

$$x \leq -2$$

One more thing to mention here: If you are given an algebraic equation that is has 0 on one side and factors with variables, set each factor to 0 to solve for the variable. For example,

Solve for x: $(2x + 6)(3x - 15) = 0$

$$2x + 6 = 0 \text{ and } 3x - 15 = 0; \; x = -3, 5$$

An algebraic function like the one above is a polynomial of degree 2, which is a quadratic. To get the degree of a polynomial, add up all the exponents in each term, and the degree is the sum of exponents in the highest term. For example, for $4x^3y^5 + 8x^8y + 4x + 5$, the degree is 9, since in the second term, which has the largest sum of exponents, the sum of the exponents is 8 + 1 = 9.

Geometry

The **geometry** section here is pretty straightforward. See the arithmetic reasoning portion of the guide for examples of perimeter and area. New information will be covered here.

Angles

Angles are typically measured in degrees. As an example, if you were to completely rotate around a circle a single time, you would have gone 360 degrees, since there are 360 degrees in a circle. Half a circle is 180 degrees, a quarter circle is 90 degrees, and so on. Degrees are used to talk about what fraction of a total rotation around a circle a certain angle represents.

Here is some terminology to keep in mind:
- ❖ **Acute angles** – Angles with a measurement of less than 90 degrees.
- ❖ **Right angles** – Angles with a measurement of exactly 90 degrees.
- ❖ **Obtuse angles** – Angles with a measurement of more than 90 degrees.
- ❖ **Complementary angles** – Two angles that add up to 90 degrees.
- ❖ **Supplementary angles** – Two angles that add up to 180 degrees.

Note that the sum of two angles that form a straight edge is 180 degrees. Note also that angles corresponding angles of parallel lines are equal.

For example:

145°   35°

Triangles

Triangles are geometric figures that have three sides (which are straight). The most important thing you need to know about triangles is that the sum of the measurements of the angles always equals 180. This is important because it means that if you know two of them, you can very easily calculate the third simply by subtracting the first two from 180. There are three types of triangles that you need to know about:

- ❖ **Equilateral triangles** – These are triangles in which the three sides and three angles are the same measure. Each one of the angles is 60 degrees, since $3 \times 60° = 360°$.

- ❖ **Isosceles triangles** – These are triangles that have two sides of the same length. The two angles that are directly opposite the sides of the same length will be the same angle. If B was the third angle, then you could state that lines between A and B (AB) and between lines B and C (BC) are the same: AB = BC.

- ❖ **Right triangles** – These might be the most important. A right triangle is a triangle that has one side that equals 90 degrees. Two sides are legs and the third side, which is directly opposite the 90-degree angle, is the hypotenuse, and is the longest one of the sides.

With right triangles, you can always remember that the lengths of the sides are related by the following equation (the Pythagorean Theorem):

$a^2 + b^2 = c^2$

Remember that c is the hypotenuse, which is the side that is opposite the right angle. It is the longest of the sides.

The area of triangles is $\frac{bh}{2}$, where the base is perpendicular (form a right angle) to the base.

Also, with right triangle with two legs that are equal, the hypotenuse is always $\sqrt{2}$ times the value of a smaller side. For right triangles with 30-60-90 angles, the hypotenuse is always twice the smaller side (side across from the 30° angle), and the other leg (across from the 60° angle) is $\sqrt{3}$ times the smaller side.

Circles

A **circle**, as you probably are already aware, is a closed curve where every single point is the exact same distance from its center. If you draw a line from the outside of the circle to the fixed point in the center, you have the radius. If you draw a line from one side of the circle straight through to the other, passing through the center point, you have the diameter. A chord is a line from one point of the circle to another, but not necessarily a diameter. By the definition of a circle, all radii (plural of radius) are equal and all diameters are equal.

For a circle, remember:

diameter = 2 × radius

You can use the radius to find out the circumference of a circle (how big it is around), by using the following formula:

C = circumference

r = radius

$$C = 2\pi r$$

Think of the circumference like the perimeter of the circle; if you were to take a piece of string all the way around a circle and measure it, this would be the circumference.

To find the area of a circle, use the following formula:

A = area

r = radius

$$A = \pi r^2$$

The area is the measurement of what's inside the circle and is written in square units.

The Coordinate System

The **coordinate system** or, sometimes, the Cartesian coordinate system, is a method of locating and describing points on a two-dimensional plane; It is a reference system. The plane is two number lines that have been laid out perpendicular to each other, with the point that they cross being origin (0, 0). The origin is the point "0" for both the x (horizontal) and y (vertical) axes. Positive and negative integers are both represented in this system.

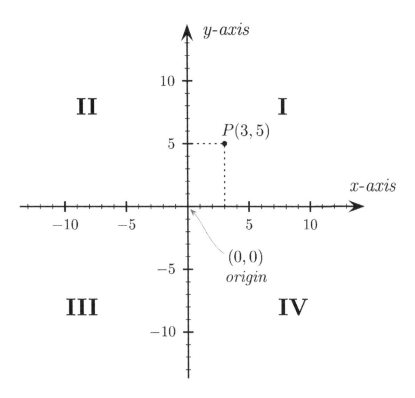

In the image above, each small tick on the line is equal to one. The larger ticks represent multiples of 5. A point is also depicted, P, which shows how things are placed onto the coordinate system. Again, the horizontal line on the coordinate plane is called the x-axis, and the vertical line on the coordinate plane called the y-axis. The points, when described, are described in reference to where they lie on that plane.

Here is an example that is the point shown above:

$$(3, 5)$$

The first number, 3, is the x-axis. The second, 5, is the y-axis. So this point is at position 3 of the x-axis (go over 3 units to the right) and position 5 of the y-axis (go up 5 units). Note that for negative x values, we go to the left that many units, and for negative y values, we go down.

A way to simplify the way these points work is to say:

$$(x, y)$$

Slope

The **slope** is the steepness of a given line. When you look on the coordinate plane, if you draw a line between two points, you will get the slope. One of the main uses of a slope is to signify a rate; it measures how much a certain thing goes up for every unit it goes over.

Here is the way to find slope:

❖ Point A: (x_1, y_1)
❖ Point B: (x_2, y_2)

103

$$\text{Slope} = \frac{(y_2 - y_1)}{(x_2 - x_1)}$$

In plain English, you will take the difference between the y coordinates and divide them by the difference between the x coordinates. Remember: y is vertical and x is horizontal.

Here is an example:

Find the slope of a line with that goes through the following points: $(9, 3)$, $(2, 12)$

First, set the problem up (always do the subtractions from the same point):

$$\frac{12 - 3}{2 - 9}$$

Next, solve the differences:

$$\frac{9}{-7}$$

So the slope of the line that goes through those two points is $-\frac{9}{7}$. You can solve this for a decimal, but there is no need to do that.

Some things to remember:

- ❖ If the slope is positive, the line is going up as it goes right.
- ❖ If the slope is negative, the line is going down as it goes right.
- ❖ The larger the absolute value (positive value) of the slope, the steeper the line.
- ❖ If a line is horizontal, its slope is 0; if a line is vertical, its slope is undefined.
- ❖ The formula for a line is $y = mx + b$, where m is the slope and b is the y-intercept (where the line crosses the y-axis).
- ❖ If two lines are parallel, they have the same slope. If they are perpendicular, they have negative reciprocal slopes.
- ❖ If two lines are intersection, the x and y values work in both equations; in other words, if you were to plug in the x and y values, both equations would be true. This is how you "solve" a system of equations.

Tips

Here are some tips to help you with the **mathematics knowledge** subtest of the SIFT:

- ❖ Make sure you read the entire question before you attempt to answer. It is extremely important to confirm what the question is actually asking you, since with multiple choice problems, they will try to trick you.
- ❖ The answer should, at a glance, make sense based on what you are asked for. If you are asked how many eggs someone is carrying home from the store, the answer is going to likely be in the range of $0 - 100$. So you can quickly eliminate any ridiculous looking answers early on.

❖ When you set up the equation that you will be using, be careful to put the correct numbers in the correct places. For example, when setting up proportions, make sure matching units are in the same spots (for example, on the left or on top).

❖ Generally, they will not give you figures if you don't need to use them. So if you see measurements and numbers in the problem, be sure to take note and figure out where you need to use them.

❖ Follow the order of operations. This shouldn't really even have to be said because it is so obvious, but always follow it. Some of the answers will likely be designed to trick you as if you hadn't done the math in the correct order.

❖ When it comes to basic arithmetic operations, you will find that practice makes perfect. The more you can practice, the easier the math problems will be. Make sure units match; for example, you may gave to convert some of the numbers from hours to minutes to match other numbers.

❖ If you can't figure out answer from the question, try each answer in the multiple choice to see if they work. In other words, you may have to work backwards for some problems.

❖ Try simpler numbers if you can't figure out the problems with the numbers given. For example, use $100 for percent problems to figure out the correct operation(s). Then apply these operations, using the more complex numbers in the problem.

❖ For word problems with variables representing real numbers, use real numbers to get an answer (to see what you're doing) and then put variables back in.

❖ Remember to utilize PEMDAS and the order of operations when you are working through problems.

❖ The more you practice, the easier the problems will be. There are a lot of internet sites with math problems.

❖ Be careful with the answers. The test will often provide common mistakes answers among the correct answer.

❖ Since you will not have access to a calculator, you will need to round π. 3.14 or $\frac{22}{7}$ are the most common ways to do this. Sometimes you may be asked to simply include it in your answer without actually utilizing the digits in your calculations at all.

❖ Don't mix up the perimeter and area formulas.

❖ One way to get good at algebra relatively quickly is to set up all of your problems, even simple ones, as algebra problems. Remember, you can simply create a variable and stick it on one side of the equation to solve for it. For example, "3 times a number added to 10 is 16" becomes "$3x + 10 = 16$". Translate almost word-for-word from English to math, and then get x by subtracting 10 from each side, and then diving by 3.

❖ Keep in mind that, unlike many tests you probably remember taking in high school, you are not being tested on your ability to write out how you solved the problem. There are many correct ways to solve mathematical problems and, as long as you come to the right answer in the end, it does not matter how you solved it. Nobody will be coming behind you and checking your scratch paper to see what you did (unless they think you are cheating, but that is a whole other ball of wax).

❖ If you can't solve the problem directly, trying plugging in the answers to see if you can figure out which one works.

❖ Pay close attention to the positive and negative signs in the work that you are doing. This is extremely important because, again, they will likely throw the correct answers out there as one of the choices but with the wrong sign.

❖ Always make sure the fractions that you are working with are simplified when you finish with them. Unless otherwise stated, the test answers will usually want the most simplified version of the fraction.

❖ Make sure you go step by step through each question. Don't skip steps or combine steps. Doing either could lead to an issue where something is accidentally missed.

❖ It might help you to change even the normal expressions into algebra. Often, understanding what you are being asked to do and knowing how to handle certain problems is only made easier when you are using algebra to handle it.

❖ Draw pictures!

Mathematics Knowledge Practice Test

1. Simplify the expression $(5x^2)^{10}$.
   A. $5^{10}x^{20}$
   B. $(5x)^{12}$
   C. $5x^{-8}$
   D. $(50x)^2$

2. Evaluate the expression $\frac{x^2-2y}{y}$ when $x = 20$ and $y = 10$.
   A. 0
   B. 38
   C. 36
   D. 19

3. Adam is painting the outside of a 4-walled shed. The shed is 5 feet wide, 4 feet deep, and 7 feet high. How much paint will Adam need if he includes the top of the shed?
   A. 126 ft^2
   B. 140 ft^3
   C. 63 ft^2
   D. 46 feet

4. Liz is installing a tile backsplash. If each tile is an equilateral triangle with sides that measure 6 centimeters in length, how many tiles does she need to cover an area of 1800 square centimeters?
   A. 36 tiles
   B. 100 tiles
   C. 50 tiles
   D. 300 tiles

5. $2.31 \times 10^2 =$
   A. 23.1
   B. 231
   C. 2310
   D. 23100

6. If $f(x) = |x - 28|$, evaluate $f(-12)$.

    A. -16

    B. 40

    C. 16

    D. -40

7. $10^8 \div 10^3 =$

    A. 10^5

    B. 10^6

    C. 10^{11}

    D. 10^{10}

8. What is 15% of 986?

    A. 146.9

    B. 98.6

    C. 9.86

    D. 147.9

9. A circular swimming pool has a circumference of 49 feet. What is the diameter of the pool?

    A. 15.6 feet

    B. 12.3 feet

    C. 7.8 feet

    D. 17.8 feet

10. 50% of 94 is:

    A. 42

    B. 52

    C. 45

    D. 47

11. If ∡A measures 57 degrees, find ∡G.

    A. 57 degrees

    B. 147 degrees

    C. 123 degrees

    D. 33 degrees

12. The table below shows the number of hours worked by employees during the week. What is the median number of hours worked per week by the employees?

Employee	Suzanne	Joe	Mark	Ellen	Jill	Rob	Nicole	Dina
Hours worked per week	42	38	25	50	45	46	17	41

    A. 38

    B. 41

    C. 42

    D. 41.5

13. Multiply the following terms: $(11xy)(2x^2y)$

    A. $13xy + x$

    B. $22x^3y^2$

    C. $44x^3y^3$

    D. $22xy^2 + 2x^2$

14. $y = 2x - 5$ and $x = 10$. What is y?

    A. 10

    B. 20

    C. 15

    D. 5

15. $x = 2, y = -3, z = 4$. Solve $x + y \times z$.

    A. −4

    B. 10

    C. −12

    D. −10

16. Factor the expression $64 - 100x^2$.

    A. $(8 + 10x)(8 - 10x)$

    B. $(8 + 10x)^2$

    C. $(8 - 10x)^2$

    D. $(8 + 10x)(8x + 10)$

17. Which expression would you solve first in the following: $(9 + 9) \times 987 + 4^6$?

    A. 4^6

    B. $(9+9)$

    C. 9×987

    D. $987 + 4$

18. Solve for y: $10y - 8 - 2y = 4y - 22 + 5y$

    A. $y = -4\frac{2}{3}$

    B. $y = 14$

    C. $y = 30$

    D. $y = -30$

19. Solve for x: $(2x + 6)(3x - 15) = 0$

    A. $x = -5, 3$

    B. $x = -3, 5$

    C. $x = -2, -3$

    D. $x = -6, 15$

20. Round 0.1938562 to the nearest tenth.

    A. 0.0

    B. 0.2

    C. 0.19

    D. 0.194

21. Points B and C are on a circle, and a chord is formed by line segment $\overline{BC}$. If the distance from the center of the circle to point B is 10 centimeters, and the distance from the center of the circle to the center of line segment $\overline{BC}$ is 8 centimeters, what is the length of line segment $\overline{BC}$?

    A. 6 centimeters

    B. 4 centimeters

    C. 12 centimeters

    D. 14 centimeters

22. If $f(x) = 3^x - 2$, evaluate $f(5)$.

    A. 27

    B. 243

    C. 241

    D. 13

23. If a spherical water balloon is filled with 113 milliliters of water, what is the approximate radius of the balloon? (Note: The volume, V, of a sphere with radius r is found using the equation $V = \frac{4}{3}\pi r^3$.)

    A. 4.0 centimeters

    B. 3.0 centimeters

    C. 3.6 centimeters

    D. 3.3 centimeters

24. Simplify $\frac{13}{26}$ into a decimal.

    A. 0.13

    B. 0.16

    C. 0.5

    D. 0.25

25. Factor the expression $100x^2 + 25x$.

    A. $100x(x + 25\,x)$

    B. $25(4x + x)$

    C. $25x(4x + 1)$

    D. $25(4x^2 + x)$

26. $F(x) = 6x - 3$, $G(x) = 3x + 4$

What will $F(3) - G(2)$ be equal to?

    A. 4

    B. 3

    C. 5

    D. 2

27. The mean of the marks obtained by the students in a class is 60 out of 100, and the standard deviation is 0. It means that:

    A. Half of the students have scored marks less than 60.

    B. Half of the students have scored marks greater than 60.

    C. No student has scored 100 marks.

    D. All the students have scored 60 marks each.

28. 0.00092×10^{-3} is equal to which of the following?

    A. 0.000093×10^{-4}

    B. 0.000092×10^{-2}

    C. 0.000000092

    D. 0.92×10^{-8}

29. The remainder is 3 when we divide one number by another number. What can be these two numbers?

    A. 9, 5

    B. 8, 5

    C. 9, 6

    D. both B and C

30. If A and B are odd integers, which of the following expressions must give an odd integer?

    A. $A \times B$

    B. $A + B$

    C. $A - B$

    D. Both A and C

31. $\frac{4}{5} \div \underline{\hspace{1cm}} = 2$

Which of the following will fill the blank?

    A. $\frac{2}{5}$

    B. $\frac{5}{2}$

    C. $\frac{1}{5}$

    D. Both A and C

32. Given a set {2, 4, 6, 8…..…50}

How many numbers in the given set are completely divisible by 3?

    A. 6

    B. 8

    C. 7

    D. 9

33. What will be the area of the shaded region in the figure below?

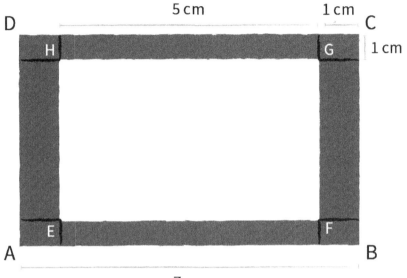

    A. 24 cm^2

    B. 26 cm^2

    C. 23 cm^2

    D. 28 cm^2

34. If $2x - y + 6 = 2$, then what is the value of $6x$?

    A. $3y + 12$

    B. $y - 12$

    C. $y + 12$

    D. $3y - 12$

35. A point is located in a coordinate system at (1, 2). What will be the location of this point if it's shifted 5 units down and 3 units to the right?

    A. (6, −1)

    B. (−4, 5)

    C. remains the same

    D. (4, −3)

36. $\dfrac{y+2}{3y^2+2y} + \dfrac{2y-1}{6y^3+4y^2} = $ ....

  A. $\dfrac{2y^2+6y-1}{6y^3+4y^2}$

  B. $\dfrac{2y^2+8y-1}{6y^3+4y^2}$

  C. $\dfrac{2y^2+6y-1}{3y^2+2y}$

  D. $\dfrac{2y^2+8y-1}{3y^2+2y}$

37. If each side of a square is increased by 1 cm, then the area is 36 cm². What was the length of one side of the square before increasing the size?
  A. 4 cm
  B. 5 cm
  C. 6 cm
  D. 7 cm

38. $(9)^{-3} = $ _____
  A. $\dfrac{1}{9}$
  B. $-\dfrac{1}{(9)^3}$
  C. $\dfrac{1}{(9)^{-3}}$
  D. $\dfrac{1}{(9)^3}$

39. What is the degree of polynomial $5x^2y - 5x^2y^2 + 5x^3y^2$?
  A. 12
  B. 4
  C. 8
  D. 5

40. Which one of the following numbers is not divisible by 3?
  A. 2352
  B. 3243
  C. 6143
  D. 5232

41. $(3-x)(3+x) = $ _____
  A. $9-x^2$
  B. x^2-9
  C. $9+x^2$
  D. x^2-6x+9

42. A car dealership is offering huge deals for the weekend. The commercials claim that this year's models are 20% off the list price, and the dealership will pay the first 3 monthly payments. If a car is listed for $26,580, and the monthly payments are set at $250, what are the total potential savings?

    A. $20,514
    B. $5,566
    C. $6,066
    D. $1,282

43. Joe baked brownies in a 9 inch × 11 inch × 2 inch tray. He then cut the brownies into 12 large pieces. Joe ate 2 pieces, his girlfriend ate 3 pieces, and his roommate, ate half of what was remaining. How much of the brownies did Joe's roommate eat?

    A. 99 in^3
    B. 57.75 in^3
    C. 82.5 in^3
    D. 115.5 in^3

44. The county is instituting a new license plate system. The new plates will have 6 digits: the first digit will be 1, 2, or 3, and the next 5 digits can be any number from 0 – 9. How many possible unique combinations does this new system offer?

    A. 3×10^5
    B. 3×10^6
    C. 10^6
    D. 53

45. What percent of 14 is 35?

    A. 4.9%
    B. 2.5%
    C. 40%
    D. 250%

46. The high temperature on Wednesday is 4° degrees warmer than the high temperature on Tuesday, which was 5° cooler than the high temperature on Monday. If the high temperature on Thursday is predicted to be 3° cooler than the high on Wednesday, what is the difference in temperature between Monday and Thursday?

    A. 3°
    B. 4°
    C. 6°
    D. 12°

47. A dry cleaner charges $3 per shirt, $6 per pair of pants, and an extra $5 per item for mending. Annie drops off 5 shirts and 4 pairs of pants, 2 of which need mending. Assuming the cleaner charges an 8% sales tax, what will be Annie's total bill?

    A. $52.92

    B. $49.00

    C. $45.08

    D. $88.20

48. A car dealership has sedans, SUVs, and minivans in a ratio of 6:3:1, respectively. In total, there are 200 of these vehicles on the lot. What proportion of those vehicles are sedans?

    A. 120

    B. $\dfrac{3}{100}$

    C. $\dfrac{3}{5}$

    D. $\dfrac{3}{10}$

49. A summer camp requires a ratio of 1 camp counselor to every 6 campers. Each camp counselor makes $480 per week. If the camp director wants to register an additional 30 campers for 2 weeks this summer, how much more will she have to budget to pay counselors?

    A. $2,400

    B. $4,800

    C. $5,760

    D. $2,880

50. Simplify: $\left(x^{1/2}\right)^{-3}$

    A. $x^{-1/2}$

    B. $x^{-5/2}$

    C. $\dfrac{1}{\sqrt{x^3}}$

    D. $\sqrt{x^3}$

1.	A.	26.	C.
2.	B.	27.	D.
3.	A.	28.	B.
4.	B.	29.	D.
5.	B.	30.	A.
6.	B.	31.	A.
7.	A.	32.	B.
8.	D.	33.	A.
9.	A.	34.	D.
10.	D.	35.	D.
11.	C.	36.	A.
12.	D.	37.	B.
13.	B.	38.	D.
14.	C.	39.	D.
15.	D.	40.	C.
16.	A.	41.	A.
17.	B.	42.	C.
18.	B.	43.	B.
19.	B.	44.	A.
20.	B.	45.	D.
21.	C.	46.	B.
22.	C.	47.	A.
23.	B.	48.	C.
24.	C.	49.	B.
25.	C.	50.	C.

Chapter Seven: Mechanical Comprehension

The mechanics section of the SIFT has a 15 minute time limit, but the number of questions varies since like the Math Skills Test, it is a computer adaptive section. It is important to note again, you cannot skip any questions, nor can you come back and change any answers. It is imperative that you do your absolute best on each question, meaning that even if you have to guess, carefully eliminate as many wrong choices as possible first.

Before diving into the topics covered in the mechanical section of the SIFT, we should first define two types of values used in physics; **scalars** and **vectors**.

In most basic math, simple numerical values are calculated (for instance 1 + 1 = 2). These simple numbers are known as **scalar** values, meaning they have a magnitude, but no direction, associated with them. Mass is an example of a scalar value commonly used in physics.

However, we live in a three-dimensional universe, so normally a simple number cannot sufficiently describe a physical characteristic. Instead, we need a magnitude as well as a direction, which is known as a **vector**. A vector not only tells how large a value is, but also whether it acts upward, to the left, to the right, etc.

For example, **speed** is a scalar value that tells you how fast an object is going. But if you are driving, knowing only the speed of your car, it will be impossible to navigate. Instead, you need to know your speed as well as the direction in which you are traveling, which is a vector value known as **velocity**. Velocity tells the direction and speed that an object is traveling.

Force and Newton's Laws of Motion

A **force** is a push or pull that can result in an object's motion or change of shape, and has a magnitude and direction, making it a vector. Force is measured in **Newtons** (N) in the metric system of units, but can also be measured in the standard unit of **pounds force** (lbf).

Though its effects can be noticed, a force cannot be seen; it can be thought of as an interaction between two bodies. The basic rules of forces are described by **Newton's Laws of Motion**, which are the foundation of the field of **mechanics**.

First Law of Motion: Until acted on by an external force, an object's velocity will remain constant, meaning speed and direction will not change. You may recognize: "An object at rest will remain at rest and an object in motion will remain in motion until a force is applied." An object's natural resistance to a change in its motion is known as **inertia**, so Newton's first law is also known as the **Law of Inertia**.

Intuitively, the law of inertia makes sense. If a soccer ball is resting in a field, it is not going to move until someone kicks it. Once the ball is kicked, though, it does not continue to travel forever, which seems like it is a violation of Newton's first law.

However, there are forces such as drag from the air and friction from the field that eventually cause the ball to come to stop again. In the same way, if a moving car is put into neutral, it will slow down and eventually stop due to parasitic losses in the car's wheels and drivetrain, aero drag, and friction.

Second Law of Motion: Describes a force's effect on the motion of a body. It states that the acceleration of the object will be proportional to the sum of the forces being applied. Algebraically, Newton's second law is written as: $F = m * a$.

Here, F is force, m is mass in kilograms (kg) or pounds mass (lbm), and a is acceleration in meters per second squared (m/s²) or feet per second squared (ft/s²). Notice that force and acceleration are both vectors, so the acceleration of an object will be in the direction of the force being applied to it.

Acceleration is defined as the rate of change of an object's velocity. Acceleration does not have to result in a change in speed; it can also cause a change in direction, as is the case in centripetal, or rotational, acceleration. Remember that velocity and acceleration are two separate and distinct values. Just because the acceleration is positive does not mean that the object's velocity is positive and vice versa.

A negative velocity would mean the object is going backward (or opposite of the direction designated as "positive") and a positive acceleration means the object's velocity is increasing in the positive direction (or decreasing in the negative direction). Though the term "deceleration" is often used to describe a decrease in speed, this is not technically correct. Instead, a change in velocity is always called acceleration and can either be positive or negative, depending on direction.

Third Law of Motion: Involves the coupling of forces and reactions. The law is often stated as, "For every action there is an equal and opposite reaction." The actions and reactions we are considering are forces. For example, if you lean against a wall, you are applying a force on the wall. According to Newton's third law, the wall is applying the same force back on you. These two forces will be the same magnitude, but in opposite directions; you push toward the wall and the wall pushes back on you. Because there is no motion involved when you lean again a wall, this is considered a **static** example.

A **dynamic** example of Newton's third law is two cars crashing. If one car collides into a second, stationary car, both cars feel the same amount of force. The force applied to the stationary car is in the direction of the collision and causes the car to begin moving in the same direction as the first car. The moving car would have a force applied to it in the opposite direction by the stationary car, resulting in, among other things, a decrease in speed. Since the force on the two cars will be in opposite directions, the acceleration of the cars will also be in opposite directions; the stationary car speeds up and the moving car slows down.

BEFORE   AFTER

Collision of a car moving at velocity V_1 into the second stationary car with the force car 1 applies on car 2 F_1, the equal force car 2 applies on car 1 F_{21}, and the resulting accelerations a_1 and a_2.

Centrifugal Force

The terms centripetal and centrifugal force are often incorrectly used interchangeably. A **centripetal force** is a force that makes an object travel along a curved path. This means a centripetal force creates a **centripetal acceleration** toward the center of the curved path.

For example, when a car is driven in a circle, the front tires exert a centripetal force on the car, accelerating it toward the center of the circle. Passengers in the car feel as though they are being pulled toward the outside of the circle, and this pull is **centrifugal acceleration**, which results from **centrifugal force**.

A centrifugal force is the reaction force of a centripetal force that pulls an object toward the outside of the curved path being traveled. This all means that a centrifugal force and a centripetal force are of equal magnitude and opposite directions, just as would be expected of a force and reaction according to Newton's third law. As Newton's second law states, centripetal force equals the mass of the object multiplied by centripetal acceleration:

$$F_c = m \times a_c = m \times v^2/R$$

Here, a_c is the centripetal acceleration and is equal to the square of the object's linear velocity (v) divided by the radius of the curved path, R.

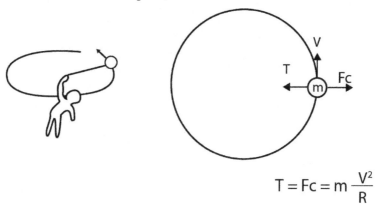

$$T = Fc = m\,\frac{V^2}{R}$$

When a ball on a string is swung in a circle, the string exerts a centripetal force on the ball, preventing it from leaving the circular path, and the resulting centrifugal force pulls the ball outward, causing tension in the string and keeping it taut.

The Law of Gravity and Weight

Sir Isaac Newton also formulated the **law of universal gravitation**. Although it is not considered one of Newton's three laws of motion, this is a very important law of physics and has profound implications in our world. Many people are familiar with the story of Isaac Newton observing a falling apple and coming up with the idea of gravity.

Though the authenticity of this story, and even whether Newton was the original formulator of the law, is unclear, Newton's law of universal gravitation is nonetheless named after him, and it describes the mutual attraction between celestial bodies, such as planets and stars. It states that the **gravitational force** two bodies exert on each other is proportional to their masses and inversely proportional to the square of the distance between them:

$$F_g = G \times m_1 \times m_2 \, r^2$$

Here, G is the **universal gravitation constant** ($6.674 * 10^{-11}$ Nm^2/kg^2), m_1 and m_2 are the masses of the two bodies, and r is the distance between them. You may notice that there is no vector on the right side of this equation. The product of scalar values cannot equal a vector because no direction is specified, so this equation is not technically correct.

This is because the right side of this equation normally has a unit vector with a length of 1 in the direction of the measurement of the distance between the two planets. This has been left out, but remember that gravity is an attractive force; it will always tend to pull two bodies toward each other with equal force.

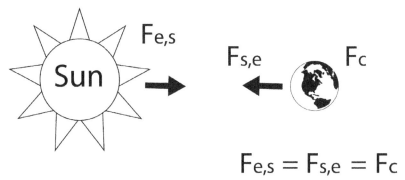

$$F_{e,s} = F_{s,e} = F_c$$

The gravitational force exerted by the sun on the Earth $F_{s,e}$ is equal to the gravitational force applied to the sun by the earth $F_{e,s}$ and is balanced (equal to) the centrifugal force resulting from the Earth's movement.

Newton's law of universal gravitation is a fairly complex concept and would seem difficult to apply to an object on the earth since there are so many objects applying a gravitational force on each other. Just look around; every object you see is applying a gravitational force on you, and you are pulling all those things toward you with the same force!

Thankfully, the law of gravity can be greatly simplified when dealing with objects on the earth's surface. The earth has a mass so much greater than any of the other objects around you that the force of gravity pulling objects toward the earth's center is much stronger than the attraction between any objects on the earth's surface. This means that we can ignore all gravitational forces besides the earth's gravity, which proves accurate when making calculations except in very rare cases, such as when a person is standing next to the Himalayan Mountains. (Next to the Himalayan Mountains, a plumb line will not point directly toward the center of the earth, but skew slightly toward the mountains, but even in this case the error in measurements is small.)

Another simplification arises from the huge radius of the earth. No matter how good of an arm you have, if you throw a ball into the air, it will not go very far at all when compared to the earth's radius. This means that even if you take an elevator to the top of a very tall building, you really haven't changed your distance from the center of the earth, so you'll still feel approximately the same gravitational force.

Therefore, we can reduce the universal gravitation equation to a simple equation for the earth's force of gravity on an object:

$$F_g = m \times g$$

Here, m is the mass of the object in kilograms (kg) or pounds mass (lbm) and g is the **acceleration due to gravity**, which is 9.81 m/s² or 32.2 ft/s² towards the center of the earth. This constant acceleration of gravity near the surface of the earth means that any object, no matter what its mass, will fall to the ground at the same rate, as long as there is not significant aero drag. If a bowling ball and an orange are dropped from a building at the same time, they will accelerate toward the earth at the same rate and hit the ground at the same time.

The constant acceleration of gravity also gives rise to the concept of **weight**. The weight of an object is merely a measure of the force of gravity on the object (m * g), and is measured in Newtons (N) or pounds force (lbf).

The object's mass is a constant scalar value that cannot be changed. However, if the object is taken to another planet, its weight, which is a vector, may be different depending on that planet's acceleration of gravity. The fact that weight is a force means that an object, such as this book, resting on your table exerts a force on the table; the table exerts a force of the same magnitude, the object's weight, back on the object.

This force exerted back on the object opposing the object's weight is known as a **normal force** because it is normal, or perpendicular, to the surface of the table. If you hold this book flat in your hands, you must apply an upward force to keep the book stationary; therefore you are supplying the normal force equal to the book's weight.

Table supporting the weight of a book

Gravity exerts a force equal to the book's weight onto the table and the table exerts an normal force back on the book so the book does not fall to the ground.

Another concept arising from the idea of weight force is an object's **center of gravity** or **center of mass**. The center of mass is essentially the average location of the object and is often used in physics to simplify problems, treating the object as a single particle with all of its mass at its center of gravity.

An object's stability is also determined by the location of its center of gravity. For example, if you stand flat-footed with straight legs and try to reach for an object fairly far in front of you, you may feel off-balanced. When you lean forward and reach out your arms, you are shifting your center of gravity forward in front of your feet, creating a torque that will cause you to fall forward once it is too great for your feet to overcome.

However, if you either bend your knees or stick one of your legs out behind you as you reach forward, the extra weight behind your grounded foot counteracts the weight in front of your foot so that your center of gravity does not shift, keeping you balanced.

This is very similar to a crane that has a large weight just behind the operator's cab to counteract added weight on the crane's arm when lifting. This weight's position is often adjustable, so it can be moved farther away from the crane's base when picking up objects that are either heavy or near the end of the crane's arm; without this large counterweight, a crane could not lift heavy objects without tipping over.

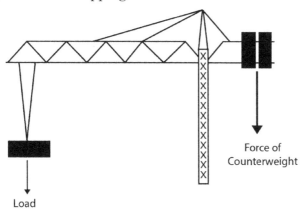

Force of
Counterweight

Load

Torque

Torque (twisting force which attempts to rotate an object), or **moment** due to a force, equals the distance of the force from the **fulcrum**, or pivot point, multiplied by the tangential force:

$$T = F_x r.$$

F is the force and r is the **torque arm**, or distance from the fulcrum.

In the crane example, the middle of the crane acts as a fulcrum and the counterweight and load apply forces downward, creating two moments in opposite directions; the load is twisting the crane counterclockwise and the counterweight twists clockwise. Torque is measured in Newton-meters (Nm) or foot-pounds-force (lbf-ft).

It is important to remember that the force and distance are both vectors, which means that the component of force and the torque arm considered must be perpendicular. Applying force to the handle of a wrench is another example.

If the 10lbf force is applied to a 10-inch wrench, then the torque on the bolt is 100 in-lbf. If the force is not applied at a 90 degree angle, the resulting torque will not be as high. For instance, if the force is applied at a 30 degree angle to the wrench handle, then the component of the force perpendicular to the wrench is only 5 lbf, and the resulting torque is just 50 in-lbf.

Friction

The normal force created by gravity also gives rise to a resistance to sliding known as **friction**. If you try to slide a refrigerator across a floor, you may find it very hard to move the object. Newton's third law suggests that there must be a force opposing your attempts to push the refrigerator; if not, it would easily slide across the floor and continue to slide until acted on by another force, such as a wall. This force opposing your efforts to move the refrigerator is friction. There are two types of friction: static and kinetic.

As you might have guessed, **static friction** is the force of friction between two objects that are not moving relative to each other. Static friction arises from the attempt to slide two surfaces past each other. In our refrigerator example, there is no force of friction until you attempt to push the refrigerator.

If you are not applying a force on the refrigerator, the only forces felt by the refrigerator are the force of gravity and the normal force of the floor holding it up, both of which are equal to the refrigerator's weight. When you start to push on the refrigerator and it does not move, static friction is holding the refrigerator in place.

The force of static friction is equal to the force that you are applying to the refrigerator; however, once pushed hard enough, the refrigerator will begin to move. The force necessary to start sliding an object is called **stiction** and is given by the equation: $F_{f,s} = \mu_s * N$.

$F_{f,s}$ is the maximum force of static friction (stiction), N is the normal force applied on the object by the surface across which it is sliding, and μ_s is the **coefficient of static friction**. Past this stiction point, the object will begin to move, and the force of **kinetic friction** will oppose the sliding motion: $F_{f,k} = \mu_k * N$. This is the same as the equation for static friction, except that the coefficient μ_k is the **coefficient of kinetic friction**.

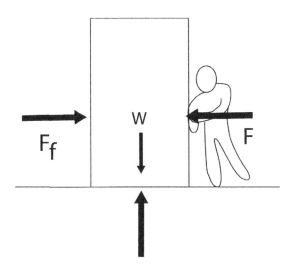

The force of friction, whether static or kinetic, will always oppose the direction of the force causing the sliding. Also, both coefficients of friction are always less than one, and the coefficient of static friction is usually greater than the coefficient of kinetic friction.

This means that it takes a greater force to get an object to start sliding across a surface than it does to keep the object sliding once it has already started. The figure following shows a graph of the force of friction versus the sliding force applied to an object.

Considering this graph in relation to our refrigerator example, if you start pushing on the refrigerator, the force of static friction will prevent sliding until you have applied enough force to overcome the stiction point. After this, the force of kinetic friction will give a constant opposition to the sliding, no matter how hard or fast you push.

Force of Friction (F_f) with Increasing Applied Force (F)

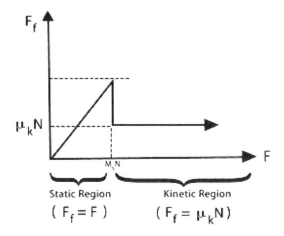

Energy

An object raised to a height above the ground will have an amount of stored energy known as **gravitational potential energy**. The higher an object is moved, the more potential it has. Gravitational potential energy is defined as:

$$PE = m \times g \times h.$$

Here, m is the mass of the object, g is the acceleration of gravity (9.81 m/s^2), and h is the height of the object from the surface of the earth.

Sometimes, gravitational potential energy is represented by the letter U instead of PE.

Gravitational potential energy, like all types of energy, is given in units of joules (J) or foot-pounds-force (ft-lbf). You may notice that gravitational potential energy is simply the force of gravity on an object multiplied by the objects height.

Since the force of gravity, or weight, is given in units of Newtons, one joule is the same as one Newton multiplied by one meter (1J = 1Nm). When an object is dropped, its gravitational potential energy is converted into **kinetic energy**, which is defined as: KE = ½ m * v^2.

Here, m is again the mass of the object and v is the object's velocity.

Kinetic energy also has units of joules and is sometimes represented by the letter E instead of KE. Energy is always conserved, meaning it cannot be created or destroyed. This is known as the law of **conservation of energy**. The law of conservation of gravitational energy can be written as:

$$PE + KE = m \times g \times h + \tfrac{1}{2} m \times v^2 = \text{constant.}$$

However, all types of energy are always conserved, whether mechanical, electrical, chemical, nuclear, solar, etc. Even the power plants that supply our homes with electricity do not create energy; they simply convert kinetic, chemical, nuclear, or solar energy into electrical energy.

If an object is brought to a certain height, it has a particular amount of gravitational potential energy. When the object is dropped, its potential energy is converted to kinetic energy, so the amount of gravitational potential energy that the object had at its highest point will be exactly how much kinetic energy it has as it hits the ground (ignoring aero drag).

The law of conservation of energy applies to all objects in a gravitational field, so the velocity of a falling object will depend only on the height through which it has fallen and not the path. This means that the same laws used to find the speed of a falling baseball can also be used to find the speed of a rollercoaster.

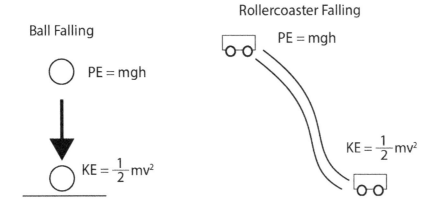

Work

In physics, the term **work** refers to a force applied over some distance: $W = F \times d$.

F is the force being applied, and d is the distance of movement in the direction of the force.

It is important to remember that the distance measured is the **displacement** in the direction of the force, which is not the same as total distance traveled; displacement is the distance between the starting and ending points.

If you are holding a book and either keep it stationary or move it to the side, no work has been accomplished because you are pushing upward on the book and there has been no upward movement.

If you move the book upward, work has been done against gravity, and if you allow the book to move downward while holding it, you have done negative work because the movement was opposite the direction of the force you are applying.

In the case of downward movement, one can also say that gravity has done the work; the gravitational force is pulling the book downward in the same direction as the book's movement, so gravity has done positive work on the book.

Work is given in units of joules (J) or foot-pounds-force (ft-lbf). This is the same unit as energy because work can also be thought of as a change in the state of energy of an object, known as the **work-energy theorem**.

In our example of the book, if it weighs 1N and you lift it 1m upward, you have done 1 J of work, or added 1 J of gravitational potential energy. You can verify this by comparing the equations for work and potential energy. Since the force you are exerting to hold up the book is equal to the weight of the book, the work equation is the same as the equation for gravitational potential energy ($m * g * h$).

Power

Power is the rate at which work is done: $P = W/t$.

W is the amount of work done in joules (J) and t is the time over which the work was accomplished in seconds (s). One joule per second (J/s) is equal to a watt (W), the common metric unit of power.

Power can also be given in units of foot-pounds-force per second (ft-lbf/s) or horsepower (hp). One horsepower is equal to 550 ft-lb/s or 746 W. Work is force times distance, so if a force is being applied to an object to move it at a constant velocity, we can also say that power is force times velocity:

$$P = F \times d/t = F \times v.$$

F is force, and v is velocity either in meters per second (m/s) or feet per second (ft/s).

Simple Machines

These physics definitions of work and power can be counterintuitive. If you hold dumbbells in front of you with your arms outstretched, you will eventually grow tired. However, if the weights are not moving, according to the laws of physics, no work has been done and, no matter how long you hold the weights, no power will ever be used. Your physical exhaustion results not from the work done, but the force you have to apply to hold the weights in place.

This is the basis for the simple machines that we use to make our lives easier every day. **Simple machines** are devices that change the direction or magnitude of a force. The **mechanical advantage** of simple machine is defined as the output force divided by the force that is applied: $MA = F_{out}/F_{in}$.

F_{out} is the machine's output force or load and F_{in} is the force input or effort to the simple machine. The mechanical advantage is, in a sense, the percentage of the input force that is applied as the output of the simple machine. A simple machine does not do work or create power, instead work and power are said to be conserved, meaning that a simple machine can multiply force only by sacrificing displacement and speed.

Levers

The first type of simple machine we will look at is the lever. A **lever** is simply a beam with a pivot or hinge known as a **fulcrum**, which can either multiply the input force by sacrificing output travel distance or multiply distance and speed with a decreased output force. The mechanical advantage of lever is given by: $MA_{lever} = d_{in}/d_{out}$.

Here, d_{in} is the distance from the fulcrum to the point where the input force is applied, or input arm, and d_{out} is the output arm, or distance from the fulcrum to the point of the output force. Levers are divided into three types or classes: **first class**, **second class**, and **third class**.

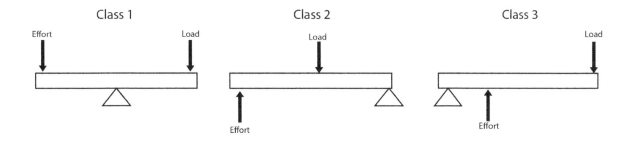

Class 1 Class 2 Class 3

When an input force is applied to a lever, it creates a moment, or torque, about the fulcrum, which is then balanced by the output force. This means the input force multiplied by the input arm is equal to the output force multiplied by the output arm.

1. **First Class Lever**: The fulcrum is between the input and output forces, which are in opposite directions. A popular example of a first class lever is a seesaw. On a seesaw, when one person is in the air, their weight is applying a downward force on one end of the lever and the other person must apply an upward force to bring them back to the earth. A seesaw has input and output arms of equal length, so the mechanical advantage is one, meaning the input and output force and the distances traveled by the two riders are equal.

   A first class lever like this is said to have no mechanical advantage, or a mechanical advantage of one, because it merely changes the direction of the input force. If it is desired to multiply the input force, the input arm should be lengthened. This will give the lever a mechanical advantage greater than one.

   Conversely, by lengthening the input arm, the output force will not move as far. If the output arm is longer, it will move faster and farther than the input arm, but a greater input force is required. A lever like this would have a mechanical advantage less than one.

2. **Second Class Lever**: The input and output forces are on the same side of the fulcrum, with the output force closer to the fulcrum, meaning that a second class lever will always have a mechanical advantage greater than one. The most popular example of a second class lever is a wheelbarrow. The front wheel of a wheelbarrow acts as its fulcrum and the user lifts far behind the location of the load in order to lift very heavy objects.

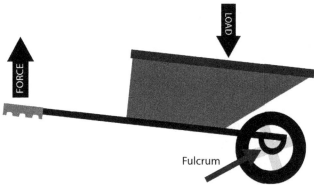

3. **Third Class Lever:** The input and output forces are on the same side of the fulcrum on a **third class lever** as well. In contrast to a second class lever, the input force of a third class lever is applied closer to the fulcrum than the load.

This means third class levers have a mechanical advantage less than one and are used to increase the output distance or speed. For example, take a swinging baseball bat: The batter places both hands near the end of the handle and swings; the top hand moves faster than the other, so the slower hand acts as a fulcrum. The end which makes contact with the ball is moving very quickly when the ball is hit.

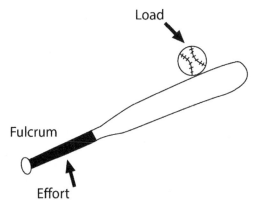

Inclined Planes

The **inclined plane** is another simple machine. Basic inclined planes are often used to do work against gravity, as is the case with a ramp. When an inclined plane is used to move an object upward, the user does not have to use as much force as if they lifted the object vertically upward.

However, the user must apply the force over a greater distance, so the work required is the same for both cases if we ignore friction. The mechanical advantage of an inclined plane is: $MA_{\text{inclined plane}} = L/H$.

L is the length of the inclined plane and H is the height, as shown in the figure below. This equation can be confusing when compared to our original mechanical advantage equation ($MA = F_{out}/F_{in}$), but in the case of an inclined plane, we can think of the output force as the force required if the load were lifted vertically upward, and the input force as the actual effort required when using the inclined plane.

It would seem that the most efficient inclined plane would have an extremely long length because this increases the mechanical advantage. However, increasing the length not only increases the travel distance up the ramp but also the strength requirement of the plane. This is similar to breaking a stick by bending it. If you have a very long twig, it can be easily broken in half.

Once the stick has been broken in half, the shorter resulting halves will be harder to break. If the process is repeated a few times, you may no longer be able to break the stick by hand. When an inclined plane is used to lift a load, the item being lifted applies a downward force to the ramp, bending and possibly breaking it if the ramp is too long or weak.

Inclined Plane

Screws

A **screw** is a specific application of the inclined plane; it is simply an inclined plane wrapped around a cylinder. If you look closely at a single-threaded screw, a triangle can be formed out of the threading by connecting consecutive teeth. The mechanical advantage of the screw will depend on the length of the tool used to turn the screw.

A screw can also be used for lifting heavy objects with the setup shown below, known as a **screw jack**. The mechanical advantage for this assembly is: $MA_{\text{screw jack}} = 2\pi R/P$.

Here, R is the torque arm, or distance from the center of the bolt (the fulcrum) and P is the distance between two consecutive teeth on the screw threading, known as the thread's pitch.

This mechanical advantage is found by considering the total distance that the input force must travel ($2\pi R$) and the total height that the screw will rise (P) in one turn of the input torque arm. Sometimes the mechanical advantage of only the screw is given, without specifying a tool or setup used to turn the screw.

In these cases, the radius of the shaft around which the inclined plane is wrapped is used as the torque arm r in the mechanical advantage equation.

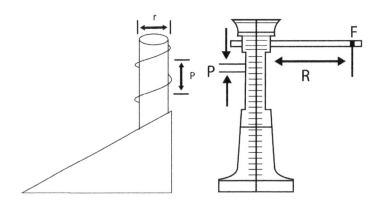

Wedges

The **wedge** is another variation of the inclined plane. A wedge can be thought of as two inclined planes placed back-to-back. Wedges are normally used for cutting and splitting as well as securing an object in place. An axe or knife is an example of a wedge used for cutting or splitting. A wedge is also used to secure the head of a hammer to its handle and to hold open doors as a doorstop. The mechanical advantage equation of a wedge differs only slightly from that for an inclined plane: $MA_{wedge} = L/t$.

The thickness, t, is measured across the end of the wedge. Again, it would seem that a wedge should be as long and sharp as possible, but a thinner, sharper wedge not only is transversely weaker (to side-loading), but also has a tendency of binding when used to chop. For instance, if a log-splitting axe is too sharp, it can become lodged in the wood with the log flexing back onto the blade, increased friction and making the axe difficult to remove.

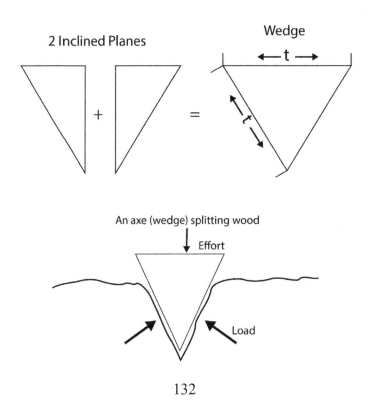

132

Pulleys and the Block and Tackle

The next type of simple machine we'll look at is the **pulley**. Pulleys are not used alone; they are used to support a cable, rope, belt, or chain, so we should discuss these items, which we will refer to simply as "cords" from now on, before trying to understand pulleys. Cords can be thought of simply as force transmitters.

However, unlike solid bodies and fluids, cords can only transmit pulling force, known as **tension**. If you try to bend or push on a cord it flexes, providing no resistance; if you secure a cord to an object and pull on it, though, it will transmit this pull as tension to the object to which it is attached.

When loaded, the tension throughout a cord is uniform, meaning that every piece of a cord along its length sees the exact same load. This is where the phrase, "A chain is only as strong as its weakest link" comes from. Each link in the chain will see the same load and be under the same amount of stress, so the entire chain can only hold the amount that the weakest link can hold before breaking.

When you pull on a rope, the force is uniformly distributed through the length of the rope as tension.

A **pulley** is a wheel and axle that supports a cord and, in doing so, changes the direction of cord's orientation and therefore the direction of the tension in the cord. Although pulleys have some frictional losses, they are small enough that we can ignore them and say that the tension in the cord is uniform. This means that the pulling force's direction is changed while its magnitude stays the same. This means that a single pulley offers no mechanical advantage (F_{in} = F_{out} so MA_{pulley} = 1).

When a pulley is used to suspend an object, the tension in the rope is uniform and equal to the weight of the object.

133

However, a series of pulleys, known as a block and tackle, can be used to give a mechanical advantage and make it possible to more easily lift heavy objects. When the input force is applied to a single cord, the mechanical advantage of a block and tackle can be found by counting the number of cord segments whose tension is being applied to lift the object: $MA_{b\&t} = N$.

Here, N is the number of cord segments extending from the moving output block, as shown in the pictures below. Again, this mechanical advantage comes at the cost of moving distance, so if the mechanical advantage is 4, then the output block will only move one quarter of the distance traveled by the input force.

The Wheel and Axle

We said that a pulley is a wheel and axle, but the wheel and axle is, in its own right, a simple machine. **Wheel and axle** refers to two cylinders that are attached to each other coaxially that are allowed to rotate about their center, as shown below. The wheel and axle can be thought of as a variation of the lever, with the fulcrum at the center and the forces applied tangentially to the surface of the wheel and the axle, sometimes using belts or rope wrapped around the wheel and/or axle. In this way, the wheel and axle creates a continuous lever. The mechanical advantage of a wheel and axle assembly is given by:

$$MA_{w\&a} = R_{wheel}/R_{axle}$$

Here, R_{wheel} and R_{axle} are the radii of the wheel and axle, respectively.

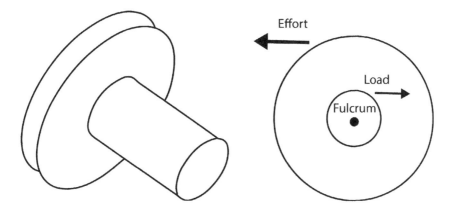

Effort

Load

Fulcrum

However, an axle does not have to have only one wheel and each wheel does not have to be the same size. The wheels on a car are the same size, but sometimes wheel and axles are required to turn various machine parts at different speeds. For this, assemblies like the one shown below are necessary. The mechanical advantage between two different wheels can be found as: $MA_{wheels} = R_{in}/R_{out}$.

Here, R_{in} and R_{out} are the radii of the input wheel and output wheel, respectively. The mechanical advantage of the wheel and axle and two-wheel assembly are both found by comparing the input and output moments about the axis; the input and output torques must be equal. Remember again that this mechanical advantage will be gained by sacrificing the distance traveled.

For instance, if the input wheel has a radius four times as large as the output, the mechanical advantage will be four. This means the output force will be four times as large as the input, but the circumference of the output wheel is a quarter of that of the input wheel, so a belt attached to the output wheel will turn only a quarter as far as one attached to the input wheel.

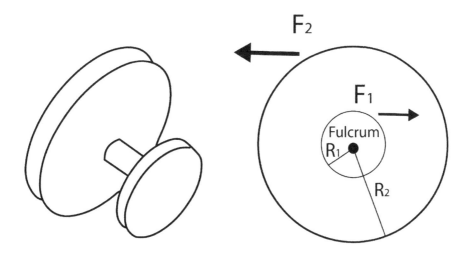

F_2

F_1

Fulcrum
R_1

R_2

Gears

The rotation and torque of a wheel can be transmitted a great distance by connecting two wheels with a belt or chain, as shown below The mechanical advantage of this setup is given by: $MA_{gears} = R_{out} / R_{in}$.

R_{out} and R_{in} are again the output and input radii, respectively. Notice that this mechanical advantage is the inverse of the mechanical advantage between two wheels on the same axle (MA_{wheels}) and is denoted as MA_{gears}. The reason that a belt or chain assembly's mechanical advantage is represented by MA_{gears} is that this type of pulley assembly is the same basic concept as two gears; it is two disks rotating with the same tangential velocity at their contact point.

However, two gears will rotate in opposite directionsThe only major difference between two meshed gears and two pulleys connected by a belt or chain is that two consecutive gears will rotate in opposite directions while the pulleys connected by a belt or chain will rotate in the same diection. **Gears** are simply interlocking wheels with their **effective radii** given by the point at which the two wheels have the same velocity.

Effective radii at two gears are given by the point at which their linear velocities are equal. Pulleys connected by a belt or chain are two discs that turn with the same velocity at their radii, just like gears, and the assembly's mechanical advantage is calculated the same way as a pair of gears. However, a pair of gears will rotate in opposite directions.

To find the mechanical advantage of a long **gear train**, or series of gears interlocked together, we only need to worry about the input and output gear radii, not the radii of the gears in between, as long as they are interlocked and not on the same shaft.

Again, if the output gear has a radius four times that of the input gear, the mechanical advantage will be four but the output gear will only rotate once for every four rotations of the input gear.

For two interlocking gears, the force applied at the effective radius, or meshing point, is the same for both gears, similar to the tension being constant throughout a rope or belt in the pulley assemblies. Since the gears are different radii, this creates different moments on the two gears.

If the input gear is driving a larger output gear, the output force is greater than the input and the assembly is called a torque-multiplier or speed-reduction assembly. If the output gear is smaller than the input, the assembly is a speed-multiplying or torque-reducing assembly.

$$MA = \frac{Ru}{R3} \; x \; \frac{R3}{R2} \; x \; \frac{R2}{R1} = \frac{R4}{R1} = \frac{R \; out}{R \; in}$$

Fluids and Hydraulics

If a force needs to be transmitted a great distance, it may not be convenient to use any of the mechanical simple machines discussed above. Instead, fluids can be used to transmit the force through hydraulic and pneumatic systems. The term fluid is not synonymous with liquid. A **fluid** is any material that conforms to the shape of its container and is not compressible, so we consider any liquid or gas to be an incompressible fluid.

In fluids, we define **pressure** as a force per unit area, given in pounds per square inch (psi); Pascals (Pa), which is the equivalent of one Newton (N) per square meter (m^2); or **inches of mercury** (in Hg), which is defined as the pressure exerted by a one-inch high column of liquid mercury.

The principle of transmission of pressure, also known as **Pascal's law**, states that pressure applied to one part of the fluid will be distributed evenly to the entire rest of the fluid. In large containers of liquid, the pressure relies on the pressure applied at the surface as well as the depth within the container, so the pressure increases deeper in the container due to the weight of the water.

However, in containers of gas or shallow containers of liquids, the effects of gravity can be ignored and the pressure is constant throughout the container. This principle is utilized in **hydraulics** through the setup shown in the picture below.

In this simplified hydraulic system, one piston is applying a pressure that is equal to the input force spread over the area of the piston's face. This pressure is distributed throughout the fluid, so the face of the second piston will see the same force per unit area. This relationship is stated mathematically as:

$$P_{in} = P_{out}$$

$$F_{in} / A_{in} = F_{out} / A_{out}$$

P_{in} is the pressure on the face of the input piston, which is the input force divided by the area of the input piston's face and is equal to the output pressure P_{out}. Since the output piston in this case is larger, the output force will be greater. For this dual-piston setup, we can define a mechanical advantage by dividing the output force by the input (the definition of mechanical advantage): $MA_{pistons} = A_{out} / A_{in}$.

Remember, this mechanical advantage is gained through decreasing the output motion, so if the output piston has an area four times that of the input, the mechanical advantage will be four, so the output force will be four times the input; however, the output piston will only move a quarter of the distance of the input piston's travel, assuming incompressibility of the fluid.

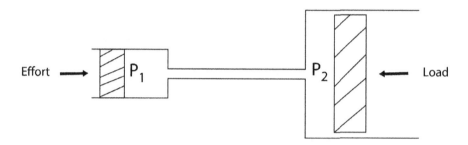

Basic Piston setup of Hydraulic System
The input force is distributed over the face of the input piston and transferred to the
fluid as pressure, which is applies an output force to the second piston.

This difference in piston motion can also be explained by considering volume displacement of the fluid. When the input piston moves, it displaces a volume of fluid equal to the area of the piston multiplied by the distance of the piston's motion.

This volume displaced causes the output piston to move to make room for the volume entering the cylinder, but since the output piston has a larger area, it will not need to move as far to displace the same amount of fluid.

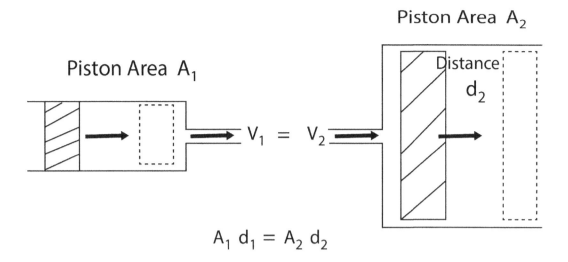

Piston Area A_1

Piston Area A_2

Distance d_2

$V_1 = V_2$

$A_1\, d_1 = A_2\, d_2$

The movement of the pistons in the hydraulic system can also be explained by fluid displacement. The volume of fluid displaced by the movement of the first piston ($V_1 = A_1 d_1$) flows into the second cylinder ($V_1 = V_2$) and causes the piston to move to make room for the incoming fluid.

This volume displacement concept can also be applied to a fluid flowing through a pipe. When a fluid is flowing through a pipe, mass must be conserved, meaning that no amount of fluid is gathering anywhere in the pipe; the amount of fluid flowing into the pipe is equal to the amount flowing out.

Since the flow is constant through all points in the pipe, the flow velocity must increase whenever the cross-sectional area of the pipe decreases. Mathematically, the law of **conservation of mass** is stated as:

$$Q_1 = Q_2$$

$$v_1 \times A_1 = v_2 \times A_2$$

Here, Q_1 and Q_2 are the volumetric flow rates of the fluid, v_1 and v_2 are the velocities of fluid particles, and A_1 and A_2 are the cross-sectional areas of the pipe at points 1 and 2, respectively.

Energy must also be conserved in the flow of a fluid, just like any other body subjected to gravity. Unlike solid bodies, however, fluids also have a defined pressure energy. This means that between any two points, the sum of a fluid's pressure, kinetic, and potential energies must remain constant. Mathematically, this is stated in a force per unit area basis:

$$p + \tfrac{1}{2}\rho v^2 + \rho g h = \text{constant}$$

$$p_1/\rho + v_1^2/2 + g h_1 = p_2/\rho + v_2^2/2 + g h_2$$

Here, p is pressure, ρ is the density of the fluid (which we assume remains constant), v is the velocity of the fluid, g is the acceleration of gravity (9.81 m/s^2 or 32.2 ft/s^2), and h is the height of the fluid.

This relationship is known as **Bernoulli's principle** and can be applied to any points along a streamline. A **streamline** is an imaginary line through a smoothly flowing fluid that is always tangential to the fluid's velocity, and can be thought of as a line that would follow the path of a particle flowing through the fluid.

Mechanical Comprehension Practice Test

1. A person moves forward ten steps and then backwards ten steps. What is the total distance traveled?
   - **A.** -10 steps
   - **B.** 0 steps
   - **C.** 10 steps
   - **D.** 20 steps

2. A springboard is a diving board made out of a flexible platform that acts like a spring and is held stationary by a hinge on one end with an adjustable fulcrum, so that a person can dive off the other end, as shown in the picture below. What will happen if the fulcrum is moved away from the diver?

Fulcrum

   - **A.** The board wil
   - **B.** The board will flex more under the weight of the diver.
   - **C.** Fulcrum position makes no difference.
   - **D.** The platform will be less likely to break.

3. A car travels 60 miles south in one hour, and then 90 miles north in two hours. What is the total displacement during this time?
   - **A.** -30 miles
   - **B.** 0 miles
   - **C.** 30 miles
   - **D.** 150 miles

4. For the car described in problem #3, what is the average speed during the first hour of travel?
   - **A.** -60 mph
   - **B.** 1 mph
   - **C.** 50 mph
   - **D.** 60 mph

5. For the car described in problem 3., what is the average speed during the 3 hours of travel?
    A. -10 mph
    B. 0 mph
    C. 10 mph
    D. 50 mph

6. For the car in problem #3, what is the average velocity during the 3 hours of travel, if we define north as the positive direction?
    A. -10 mph
    B. -1 mph
    C. 1 mph
    D. 10 mph

7. A 10 kg person stands on a scale. Approximately what will the scale read?
    A. 10 N
    B. 32 N
    C. 98 N
    D. 196 N

8. A 10 kg person travels to the Moon, which has a smaller acceleration due to gravity than the Earth. What will happen to the person's mass?
    A. The person's mass will decrease.
    B. The person's mass will stay the same.
    C. The person's mass will increase.
    D. It is impossible to tell from this information.

9. A 10 kg person travels to the Moon, which has a smaller acceleration due to gravity than the Earth. What will happen to the person's weight?
    A. The person's weight will decrease.
    B. The person's weight will stay the same.
    C. The person's weight will increase.
    D. It is impossible to tell from this information.

10. A person travels to a distant planet and finds that their weight has increased relative to their weight on Earth. Assuming the person's mass has not changed, what can we say about the planet's radius?
    A. The planet's radius is smaller than that of Earth.
    B. The planet's radius is equal to that of the Earth.
    C. The planet's radius is larger than that of the Earth.
    D. It is impossible to tell from this information.

11. What force is required to accelerate a 10 kg object from rest to 10 m/s in 5 seconds? (Assume no resistive forces.)
- **A.** 15 N
- **B.** 20 N
- **C.** 100 N
- **D.** 500 N

12. A 50 kg object begins at rest on a surface with a static coefficient of friction at 0.6 and a kinetic coefficient of friction at 0.5. If you push horizontally on the object with a force of 27 N, how quickly will it move across the surface? (Assume that the object does not tip over.)
- **A.** 0 m/s
- **B.** 5 m/s
- **C.** 20 m/s
- **D.** 30 m/s

13. Which of these best describes the gear train below?

- **A.** Torque-multiplier
- **B.** Speed-multiplier
- **C.** Frequency-multiplier
- **D.** None of the above

14. The figure below shows an air duct that narrows at a point. A U-tube is attached as shown and the bottom is filled with water. What will happen to the water when air starts flowing through the duct?

- **A.** The left side will go up and the right side will go down.
- **B.** Both sides will go down.
- **C.** The left side will go down and the right side will go up.
- **D.** Both sides will go up.

15. Which of these describes the pulley train shown below?

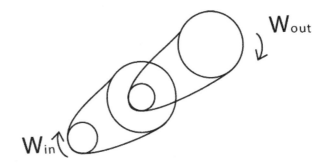

   A. Rotation-inverter
   B. Speed-multiplier
   C. Torque-multiplier
   D. None of the above

16. To have the best leverage in the scissors below, you should:

   A. Hold the scissors at D and cut at A
   B. Hold the scissors at D and cut at B
   C. Hold the scissors at C and cut at A
   D. Hold the scissors at C and cut at B

17. Which of the objects in the figure below weighs more?

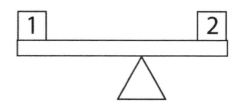

   A. Object 1.
   B. Object 2.
   C. They weigh the same amount.
   D. It is impossible to tell.

18. Which of these statements is true about a car's transmission?
- **A.** Higher gears have a higher mechanical advantage.
- **B.** Lower gears have a higher mechanical advantage.
- **C.** All the gears have the same mechanical advantage.
- **D.** The mechanical advantage depends on the weight of the car.

19. In the picture below, does the support on the left or right carry more of the object's weight?

- **A.** Left supports more weight
- **B.** Right supports more weight
- **C.** They carry the same amount of weight
- **D.** It is impossible to tell

20. Three cubes of equal volume are put in a hot oven. The cubes are made of three materials: wood, iron, and silver. Which cube will heat the fastest?
- **A.** The wooden cube
- **B.** The iron cube
- **C.** The silver cube
- **D.** The cubes all heat up at the same rate.

21. Which of block and tackle pictured below requires the least effort to lift a weight of W?

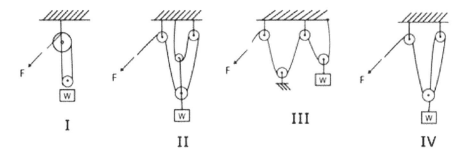

- **A.** I
- **B.** II
- **C.** III
- **D.** IV

22. What can be said about the three objects shown below in a tank of water?

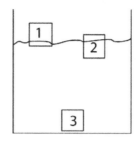

    A. Object 3 weighs the most.
    B. Object 1 has the lowest density.
    C. Objects 1 and 2 have the same density.
    D. None of the above

23. Two gears create a mechanical advantage of 4:1 and the larger gear has 24 teeth. How many teeth does the pinion have?
    A. 6 teeth
    B. 12 teeth
    C. 24 teeth
    D. 96 teeth

24. In the hydraulic system shown below, the valve is originally closed and the two objects are level. When the valve is opened, the object on the right begins to move downward and the object on the left moves upward. What can be said about the two objects?

    A. Object 1 weighs more.
    B. Object 2 weighs more.
    C. The objects weigh the same amount.
    D. It is impossible to tell from this information.

25. The figure below is a simplified model of the camshaft in a car's engine. The pulley attached to the crankshaft is of half the diameter of the pulley attached to the camshaft. About how far must the crankshaft turn before the camshaft pushes the valve all the way open?

    A. 90 degrees
    B. 180 degrees
    C. 270 degrees
    D. 540 degrees

26. The picture below shows a hinged arm attached to a weight and being held horizontal by a spring. If the weight is moved to the left (closer to the hinge), what will happen?

    A. The spring will compress more.
    B. The spring will extend.
    C. Nothing
    D. It is impossible to tell.

27. The picture below shows an axe splitting a piece of wood. What type of simple machine is this?

    A. Lever
    B. Blade
    C. Inclined plane
    D. None of these

28. The picture below shows a person lifting a heavy object with a lever. What is the mechanical advantage?

    A. 0.25
    B. 0.3
    C. 3
    D. 4

29. Which of these best describes the gear train shown below?

    A. Torque-multiplier
    B. Speed-multiplier
    C. Frequency-multiplier
    D. None of the above

30. If the input gear on the top has the same diameter as the input pulley on the bottom and the output gear on the top has the same diameter as the output pulley on the bottom, which assembly gives the higher mechanical advantage?

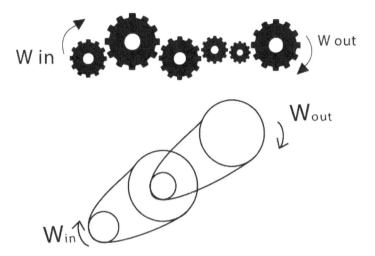

   A. The gear train on the top.
   B. The pulley train on the bottom.
   C. The assemblies have the same mechanical advantage.
   D. It is impossible to tell.

Mechanical Comprehension Practice Test Answer Key

1. **D. 20 steps**. Total distance traveled does not take direction into account, so we can add the two distances: $10 + 10 = 20$ steps.

2. **B. The board will flex more under the weight of the diver**. The distance between the fulcrum and the diver is being lengthened, so the torque arm is being increased; the weight of the diver will apply a greater moment to the platform, resulting in the platform flexing a greater amount.

   You can also consider the two extremes of the fulcrum either being adjusted directly underneath the diver or as far away from the diver as possible. If the fulcrum is underneath the diver the board will not flex at all, and if the fulcrum is the farthest point away from the diver the board will flex the maximum amount.

   This means that the board flexes more as the fulcrum is adjusted away from the diver. Since the board is flexing more, it would be more likely to break because there is a greater moment.

3. **C. 30 miles**. Displacement is the distance between the starting and ending points, so we cannot simply add the two distances together. If we take north as the positive direction, the car moves 60 miles in the positive direction and then 90 miles in the negative direction.

   Adding these values, $60 + (-90) = 60 - 90 = -30$ miles. However, displacement is always positive. Displacement is not a vector, but a scalar. It is just the distance between the start and end points, NOT the vector distance between the two points.

4. **D. 60 mph**. Speed is distance traveled divided by time and does not take direction into account. In this case, the car travels 60 miles in one hour, 60 miles / 1 hour = 60 miles per hour.

5. **D. 50 mph**. Speed is a scalar value, so it does not take direction into account. Average speed is distance traveled divided by time (x/t), so we first find the distance traveled, $60 + 90 = 150$ miles, then the total time, $1 + 2 = 3$ hours, and finally divide the distance by time, $150/3 = 50$ miles per hour.

   While it is also possible to find the average speed during the two legs of the trip and calculate a weighted average, this is much more complicated and reduces to the same equation.

6. **D. 10 mph**. Notice in this question we have to define a positive direction because the question asks for a vector value, which has a magnitude and direction. Similar to

150

problem #4, we must first find the total displacement of the car, which is 30 miles. Remember that this is north, which has been defined as the positive direction.

Like average speed, average velocity is distance divided by time, 30 miles/3 hours = 10 mph, and since the distance traveled is in the positive direction, the average velocity will also be positive: +30/3 = +10mph.-30

Again, we could also find the average velocity during each leg of the trip and find a weighted average, but this is even more complicated when working with vector values and still reduces to the same equation of total distance divided by total time.

7. **C. 98 N**. A scale measures weight, and since it is the earth's gravitational pull on the object which is being weighed, the force of gravity is the mass of the object times the constant acceleration due to gravity (9.8 m/s^2). W = mg = 10 * 9.8 = 98 N

8. **B. The person's mass will stay the same**. Mass is a scalar vector depends on the density and volume of an object, both of which will stay constant. A person's mass will stay the same no matter what planet they are on.

9. **A. The person's weight will decrease**. Weight is a measurement of force, so it is a vector value which has a magnitude that depends on mass and acceleration. We already found in problem #8 that the person's mass will not change, so their weight will be proportional to the acceleration of gravity.

   Since the acceleration due to gravity on the moon is less than that of the earth, the acceleration of gravity will decrease when the person travels to the moon, meaning their weight will also decrease.

10. **D. It is impossible to tell from this information**. Since the person's weight has increased, the acceleration of gravity on this distant planet is higher than that on Earth. It is tempting to say this must be a smaller planet. However, we cannot say anything about the planet's radius because gravitational force depends on both the mass and distance from the center of an object.

    Acceleration due to gravity on a planet depends on the planet's mass and radius; it varies directly with mass and proportionally to the inverse square of the radius (m/r^2). If this planet has the same mass as the Earth, its radius must be smaller so that the planet is denser than the earth. If the radius of the planet is the same as the Earth's, it must have a larger mass and density. However, we are not given any of this information, so the only thing we can say is that the value of m/r^2 for the planet is larger than the Earth's.

11. **B. 20 N**. This problem involves Newton's second law ($F = ma$). To find the force required, we must first calculate the desired acceleration, which is the rate of change of velocity, $a = \Delta v/\Delta t = 10/5 = 2$ m/s^2. Newton's second law states that $F = ma = 10 * 2 = 20$ N.

12. A. 0 m/s. The key to this question is that the object "begins at rest". In order for an object at rest to begin moving, the maximum static friction force must first be overcome, $F_{f,s} = \mu_s * N = 0.6 * 50 = 30$ N.

Since the force being applied is less than the "stiction" force, the object will not move. The force of friction in this case is equal to the 27 N being applied. Had the force been greater than 30 N, the object would move, a kinetic friction force of $F_{f,k} = \mu_k * N = 0.5 * 50 = 25$ N would resist the motion, and the speed at steady state would be much more difficult to find.

13. B. Speed-multiplier. Remember that in a gear train it is only necessary to look at the input and output gears. Since the input gear is larger than the output, the output gear will turn faster, making this a speed-multiplying gear train.

14. C. The left side will go down and the right side will go up. Air flowing through the duct will have to speed up at the narrow portion. According to Bernoulli's principle, the pressure in the air will decrease when the speed increases, so the pressure on the right side of the U-tube will be less than the pressure on the left side. This will push the water downward in the left side of the pipe and, since the volume of the water will stay constant (the water is incompressible), the water in the right side will rise.

15. B. Torque-multiplier. Pulley trains which include a wheel and axle like this one are not as simple as gear trains; you can't just look at the input and output pulleys. Instead, you have to look at each step of the pulleys. Fortunately, both steps of this system decrease the speed and increase torque, so this assembly is a torque-multiplier.

16. B. Hold the scissors at D and cut at B. For the best leverage, the input arm should be long and the output arm should be short. This means the load should be close to the fulcrum at B and the effort should be far from the fulcrum at D.

17. B. Object 2. Object 1 is farther away from the fulcrum, giving it a greater torque arm and therefore higher mechanical advantage that object 2. Since the lever is horizontal, the moments cause by the two objects must be equal, $F_1R_1 = F_2R_2$. $R_1 > R_2$, so therefore $F_2 > F_1$.

18. B. Lower gears have a higher mechanical advantage. When driving a car, the transmission is shifted into higher gears when the car is moving faster, so the higher gears are able to produce a higher speed at the expense of torque, meaning they have less of a mechanical advantage. If a person puts a manual transmission in a high gear and tries to move a car from rest, the engine speed will drop and the engine will most likely not have enough power to start because there is not enough of a mechanical advantage. This can also break the car's clutch.

19. A. Left supports more weight. The support on the left will carry more of the object's weight. Several approaches can be taken to analyze this problem.

If the support on the left is treated as a fulcrum and the support on the right as a force, similar to a class 2 lever, the force will not have to be large because it has a high mechanical advantage.

However, if the support on the right is treated as a fulcrum and the support on the left treated as an effort force, the force will not have much of a mechanical advantage.

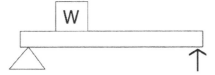

The question is analogous to finding which object weighs more on a balance, as shown below. The weight on the left represents the reaction force of the support on the left in the original question and the weight on the right represents the reaction force of the support on the right.

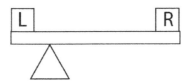

You can also think of the two extremes; if the weight is all the way to the left over the left support, the right support can be removed because it carries no load. Similarly, if the object is all the way on the right side, the right support carries the entire load. Since the object is closer to the left, the left support should carry more of the weight.

20. **C. The silver cube**. The speed at which the cubes will heat up depends on their thermal conductivity. Wood does not have a very high thermal conductivity. In metals, thermal conductivity generally follows the same trend as electrical conductivity; metals with high electrical conductivity have high thermal conductivity. This means the silver cube has the highest coefficient of thermal conductivity and will therefore heat the fastest.

21. **B. II**. Looking closely at the figure: the two pulleys above the weight in II are attached, and the weight in setup II has four rope segments extending from it, so the mechanical advantage is four and $F = W/4$. Setups I and III have two rope segments extending from the weight, giving a mechanical advantage of 2, and setup IV has three rope segments extending from it, so setup IV's mechanical advantage is 3.

22. **B. Object 1 has the lowest density**. How high an object floats in water depends on that object's density. The objects are acted on by the force of gravity, which depends on the objects mass and a buoyancy force that depends on the volume of the liquid displaced. If the question stated that the three objects had the same volume, then object 3 would be the heaviest because it has the highest density and density is mass per unit volume. However, the problem does not state this and the height at which an object floats only gives its density.

23. **A. 6 teeth**. The pinion refers to the smaller of the two gears, so whether the mechanical advantage is 1:4 or 4:1, the pinion will have one quarter the number of teeth as the gear.

24. **D. It is impossible to tell from this information**. Though it is tempting to say object 2 weighs more, this hydraulic system gives the force applied to the piston on the right a mechanical advantage, so object 2 could actually weigh the same or less than object 1 and still push object 1 upward. Remember, the weight of object 1 is spread over a greater area, causing less pressure, while the weight of object 2 is concentrated on a smaller area and causes greater pressure.

25. **D. 540 degrees**. It is important to note first that the lower pulley attached to the crankshaft is rotating clockwise. This means that the camshaft is also rotating clockwise. The camshaft must turn 270 degrees (3/4 turn) before the cam is aligned with the valve stem so it is pushed as far down as it will go. The crankshaft turns at twice the speed of the camshaft, so it must rotate twice as far, 540 degrees (1.5 turns).

26. **B. The spring will extend**. This is a class three lever, where the weight is the load and the spring is the effort. If the weight is moved to the left, the load's torque arm is shortened and the weight has less leverage. This means the spring does not have to apply as much force and therefore expands.

27. **C. Inclined plane**. The axe in the picture is a wedge. Remember that a wedge is a type of inclined plane.

28. **D. 4**. The mechanical advantage of the lever is the length of the input arm divided by the length of the output arm (d_{in}/d_{out}), but the two lengths must be in the same units first. The input arm is two feet or 24 inches and the output arm is 6 inches, which is half a foot. Either way, $24/6 = 2/.5 = 4$

29. **D. None of the above.** Normally, it is only necessary to consider the input and output gears. However, in this gear train three consecutive gears are touching, which means that this gear train will not be able to turn since two consecutive gears should turn in opposite directions.

30. **B. The pulley train on the bottom**. The pulley system has a greater mechanical advantage. For the gear train, the mechanical advantage can be found from the diameters of the input and output gears. The pulley system has two steps, both of which

are torque-multipliers. The pulley system's input and output pulleys may have the same diameter of the gear train's input and output gears, but the wheel and axle in the pulley system give it a greater mechanical advantage.

Conclusion

At Accepted, Inc. we strive to help you reach your goals. We hope this guide gave you the information to not only score well but to exceed any previous expectations. Our goal is to keep it concise, show you a few test tricks along the way, and to ultimately help you succeed in your goals. Please let us know if we've truly prepared you for the exam and if don't mind including your test score we'd be thankful for that too! Please send us an email to *feedback@acceptedinc.com.*

Remember – Study Smarter. Score Higher. Get Accepted!

-Accepted, Inc.-

Made in the USA
Coppell, TX
27 July 2021

59585101R00090